"*The Paleo Foodie Cookbook* offers world-class gastro-tourism—but with no passport required!"

—**MICHELLE TAM**, author of *Nom Nom Paleo*

"Once again, Arsy knocks it out of the ballpark with a mouthwatering and amazing assortment of Paleo recipes..."

—**KRISTEN MICHAELIS**, founder of Food Renegade

"Arsy has a flair for turning traditional dishes into unique, sophisticated and flavorful masterpieces. If you are seeking to impress and be inspired, *The Paleo Foodie* will do just that."

—**KELLY WINTERS**, founder of Primally Inspired

"Arsy has once again proven that eating a Paleo diet doesn't mean limiting flavor. A must-buy for Paleo eaters and foodies alike."

—**RUSS CRANDALL**, founder of Domestic Man

"Having had the pleasure of eating dinner from *The Paleo Foodie Cookbook* at Arsy's very own table, I can tell you that these recipes are completely amazing."

—**KELLY BROZYNA**, founder of The Spunky Coconut

"The magic of Arsy's recipes has always been transforming simple ingredients into impressive dishes. Her everyday exotic creations will surely spice up your weeknights with fabulous new flavor combinations."

—**BILL STAYLEY AND HAYLEY MASON**, founders of the Primal Palate

"A great follow-up to Arsy's first book, *The Paleo Foodie Cookbook* is a straight-forward approach to cooking whole, real foods deliciously. From inventive and exotic recipes to new twists on classics, this book will bring out the foodie in all of us."

—**MATT MCCARRY AND STACY TOTH**, founders of Paleo Parents

THE
PALEO FOODIE
Cookbook

120 FOOD LOVER'S RECIPES FOR HEALTHY, GLUTEN-FREE, GRAIN-FREE & DELICIOUS MEALS

Arsy Vartanian,

Founder and Chef of rubiesandradishes.com and author of the bestselling *The Paleo Slow Cooker*

with Amy Kubal,

Registered Dietitian and co-author of *The Paleo Slow Cooker*

PAGE STREET
PUBLISHING CO.

PAGE STREET
PUBLISHING CO.

Copyright © 2014 Arsy Vartanian

First published in 2014 by
Page Street Publishing Co.
27 Congress Street, Suite 103
Salem, MA 01970
www.pagestreetpublishing.com

Distributed by Macmillan; sales in Canada by The Canadian Manda Group; distribution in Canada by The Jaguar Book Group.

17   16   15   14   1   2   3   4   5

ISBN-13: 978-1-62414-048-8
ISBN-10: 1-62414-048-3

Library of Congress Control Number: 2013919097

Cover and book design by Page Street Publishing Co.
Photography by Spoon Fork Bacon

Printed and bound in China

Page Street is proud to be a member of 1% for the Planet. Members donate one percent of their sales to one or more of the over 1,500 environmental and sustainability charities across the globe who participate in this program.

To my little family, Brooke & Indyanna.
I love you to the moon and back.

CONTENTS

FOREWORD BY LIZ WOLFE

Because of Arsy, I fell in love with cooking.

Those who know me will understand the full meaning of that statement. To me, "cooking" used to mean, "empty the contents of this box into a microwave-safe bowl, zap and enjoy." This was, of course, before I discovered the Paleo lifestyle; and once you discover Paleo, you don't ever want to go back. That's what happens when you finally discover the secret to clear skin, digestive healing, mental clarity and overall amazing health.

With my change in lifestyle came a whole new set of kitchen adventures—I had opened the door to a world of new, nourishing foods, and now I had to learn to cook them. The alternative: living on my limited repertoire of baked chicken, bunless burgers and scrambled eggs.

Beyond the basics, cooking has always terrified me. Although I love real, nourishing food, and as a nutritional therapy practitioner and health blogger I especially love to talk about all the myths surrounding perfectly healthy foods, such as red meat, natural fats and other Paleo staples as I did in my book *Eat the Yolks*, I simply am not all that kitchen savvy. Heat, knives and frustration just don't mix well for me. My dislike for cooking persisted until I got my hands on Arsy's first book, *The Paleo Slow Cooker*. There's no better introduction to flavorful yet low-maintenance Paleo cooking than that book. It carried me through countless delicious meals. And now, with *The Paleo Foodie Cookbook*, Arsy has helped me transition from cautious slow-cooker aficionado to an enthusiastic wannabe chef with the gumption to try new combinations, flavors and cooking techniques. I'm loving every savory, sweet, delicious minute!

It's not surprising that Arsy has created yet another phenomenal cookbook. Arsy is passionate about Paleo cooking, and even more passionate about sharing the joy she takes in nourishing her family with wholesome food. I have respected Arsy as a writer, a chef, a mom and a business-woman for quite some time, and as our friendship has grown, I've continued to learn so much from her. The marvelous book you have in your hands, *The Paleo Foodie Cookbook*, is more than a cookbook—it's a lesson in appreciative eating, with recipes everyone will enjoy, including the most adventurous nose-to-tail eater; it's replete in the rich flavors of Arsy's heritage; and it's stacked with information on how to make Paleo eating healthy, affordable, and enjoyable.

There is so much to love about this cookbook and the fabulous woman who wrote it. I know you will enjoy!

—Liz Wolfe

PREFACE

For as long as I can remember, I have loved to cook. I grew up watching my grandmother and my mom spend most of the day in the kitchen, preparing traditional Middle Eastern dishes from scratch. Looking back on these dishes now, I realize many of them were innately Paleo, as many traditional foods are. Typical meals in our home consisted of stews made of meat, vegetables, spices and broth that simmered all day.

In seventh grade, I chose "Foods" for my alternative class. That semester, I came home and made every single recipe that we were taught. I vividly remember re-creating chicken enchiladas, pancakes and Rice Krispies treats. What I remember even more is how proud I felt when my family gathered for dinner, enjoying the meal that I had made for them. Later, in my vegetarian days, I would make my college roommates hefty salads with everything and anything available in the kitchen. I discovered early on that in cooking for others, I experienced a deep-rooted satisfaction.

Somewhere in my early 20s, I temporarily lost my love of cooking. This was largely due to my deteriorating health. I loved to cook, but I never felt well after I ate. I felt lethargic and foggy headed, although I was following all of the typical conventional health advice. This left me feeling confused about cooking. I was eating all of the right things (or so I thought) and making home-cooked meals, but after eating I physically felt as if I had eaten a meal straight from the drive-through window. Eventually, this led me to lose my joy of cooking and resort to making quick meals like simple salads and sandwiches.

When I started CrossFit in 2008 and learned about the Paleo diet, my passion for cooking was reignited to the utmost degree. I am just as grateful to the Paleo diet for reawakening my love of cooking as I am for it helping me regain my health. There are few things more disappointing in life than losing pleasure in your passions.

Making Paleo meals allows me to cook with clarity and confidence. I find great pleasure and satisfaction in cooking with ingredients with integrity that will nourish others. I have found that the best way to encourage others to live more healthful lives is to share with them the pleasure of a delicious and healthy meal.

Most of the recipes in this book are not intended for quick weeknight meals (although there are a few that will work for that). They are intended for you to relax, put on your favorite music and enjoy the cooking process!

Happy Cooking!
Arsy

INTRODUCTION BY AMY KUBAL, RD

THE PALEO DIET IN A (COCO)NUTSHELL

"Eat like a caveman." It sounds simple, right? But do any of us really know what our ancestors ate? We can't be 100 percent sure about everything but one thing is certain: They weren't eating the packaged, processed, unpronounceable-ingredient-containing foods that are now everyday food. There were no grocery stores, no refrigeration, no butylated hydroxytoluene, polysorbate 60, Yellow #5 or fast-food drive-through windows. Food had to be hunted and gathered every day, so food was fresh, preservative free and needed to be processed by hand (e.g., mammoth butchering and nut shelling). Even though living like a true caveman in today's world is next to impossible, we can follow their basic eating principles. If it lives, grows, rots and dies, or if it had eyes and a face, it's "fare" game.

The Paleo way of eating is based on real and whole foods. In the lives-grows-rots-and-dies category are vegetables and fruits of all kinds. (French fries and gummy fruit-flavored snacks don't count.) Ethically raised meats, poultry, wild caught fish and seafood fill the "eyes and a face" stipulation. Additionally, healthy fats sourced from coconut, olives, grass-fed animals (lard), and moderate amounts of nuts are also important components of Paleo meals. One of the many benefits of eating a diet consisting mainly of these foods is that it is anti-inflammatory, which means our bodies don't react or mount an immune or other harmful response when these foods are eaten.

The foods that are not included in a Paleo eating plan tend to be pro-inflammatory and many people have either full-out allergies to or low-level intolerances to them. The list includes gluten, wheat and all grains; dairy products; soy; legumes; processed foods; foods with concentrated or high amounts of sugar/sweeteners; vegetable oils; and alcohol. Eating this way may sound like a harsh sentence but it will make you feel so good. In time you won't miss the foods you now think you can't live without.

WHAT'S IN IT FOR ME?

The Paleo lifestyle may look a lot different from what is considered normal but the health benefits and the way you'll feel once you make the switch are well worth it. Eating a variety of real and whole foods provides the body with all of the nutrients it needs to keep running like a well-oiled machine. No more cheap gas! The body can't be traded in for a newer model. This machine requires premium fuel!

Paleo eating can prevent or be an important adjunct in treating many of the health problems that seem inevitable today: diabetes, obesity, heart disease, autoimmune diseases. Additionally, this style of eating can improve blood lipid profiles, stabilize blood sugar levels, aid weight loss, clear up skin rashes and acne, reduce allergies, improve sleep, increase energy, reduce pain and increase performance. The Paleo diet's anti-inflammatory nature and nutrient-rich profile make it a healthy and wise approach for nearly everyone.

THAT SOUNDS GREAT BUT . . .

Paleo eating sounds really good in theory, right? But making it work in a world that has fast-food restaurants on every corner and where soda is more common than water seems like a daunting task! The easiest way to make the transition is to clean out the kitchen. Get rid of everything that doesn't fit the Paleo mold: processed foods, grains, dairy, soy, legumes and any and all foods that contain these things. If less-than-optimal foods are out of the picture, turning to them in a moment of weakness is impossible! Make a menu plan. Decide ahead of time what you're going to eat for breakfast, lunch and dinner for the next day, week or month. Include new recipes and lots of variety to keep things fresh and to ensure that you're getting all the nutrients your body needs. Next, go shopping! Stock up on all of the foods you'll need to make it through the next few days or the week. Look for grass-fed meats, fresh seasonal produce and healthy fats. Prepare as much food as you can ahead of time: chop vegetables, cook extra protein, freeze soups and stews. Planning and preparation are crucial for making a Paleo lifestyle work. Once you fall into a groove, this stuff will become second nature.

DIFFERENT STROKES FOR DIFFERENT FOLKS: THE AUTOIMMUNE PALEO PROTOCOL

A Paleo lifestyle can be life changing for many, but there are some cases that call for a little fine-tuning in order to see the best health improvements. Autoimmune diseases like multiple sclerosis, rheumatoid arthritis, Hashimoto's thyroiditis, lupus, type 1 diabetes, Addison's disease and many others are serious health issues. There are many people who have been able to control and even reverse some of the symptoms of their autoimmune conditions by following an autoimmune Paleo protocol. Let's look at the differences between a standard Paleo diet and an autoimmune Paleo approach:

The autoimmune protocol may not be something that needs to be followed for life, but eliminating these other foods for a period of 30 days or until symptoms relieve is advised. Following the elimination period foods may be added back one at a time to test tolerance levels. For example, peppers might be fine but tomatoes and eggs bring symptoms back, or eggs are okay but nuts and coffee are no-gos. Everyone is different and responds differently. The only way to find out if something works for you is to try it.

FOODS TO AVOID

PALEO PROTOCOL	AUTOIMMUNE PALEO PROTOCOL
Wheat	Wheat
Grains (quinoa, oats, spelt, etc.)	Grains (quinoa, oats, spelt, etc.)
All Dairy	All Dairy
Soy	Soy
Legumes	Legumes
Processed Packaged Foods	Processed Packaged Foods
High Amounts of Added Sugars	High Amounts of Added Sugars
Alcohol	Eggs (Whites and Yolks)
	Nightshade Vegetables (tomatoes, bell peppers, hot peppers, eggplant, tomatillos, white potatoes)
	Nightshade-containing Spices and Products (paprika, curry, chili powder, cayenne, tomato sauce, salsa, etc.)
	Nuts and Seeds
	Alcohol
	Coffee
	Cocoa

THE PIPES ARE LEAKY!
THE HOWS AND WHYS BEHIND THE HOLES

Leaky gut: It's exactly what it sounds like and is the result of damage to the intestinal lining. This damage can be caused by a number of things including chronic inflammation, food sensitivity, a compromised immune system, excessive alcohol consumption, certain antibiotics and other drugs, radiation and/or regular use of NSAIDs (nonsteroidal anti-inflammatory drugs such as ibuprofen and aspirin).

When the gut is damaged or "leaky" it is unprotected from the outside environment of the body, which affects its ability to absorb and filter nutrients. Additionally, the holes in the intestinal lining allow waste and bacteria out of the gut and into the bloodstream. The presence of these unfamiliar substances in the bloodstream and other parts of the body set off an autoimmune response. This often results in bloating, gas, abdominal cramping, food sensitivities, skin rashes, fatigue and the onset of autoimmune diseases.

When a pipe is leaking in your house you call the plumber and get it fixed. When your gut has leaks, an autoimmune Paleo diet can serve as your plumber. This way of eating eliminates inflammation-triggering foods to prevent further damage, which helps to mitigate the immune response. Additionally, many foods that are included in this way of eating have gut-healing benefits. Bone broths and fermented foods are excellent tools for restoring gut health.

HOLY MACRO(S)

All of the foods that we eat contain nutrients. There are two classes of nutrients: macronutrients (carbohydrates, proteins, fats) and micronutrients (vitamins and minerals). The macronutrients are the energy-containing, calorie-containing nutrients that fuel the body. Each of the three macronutrients has different functions in the body. Balancing them is key to health.

CARBOHYDRATES

Carbohydrates are the main and most easily utilized energy source. All of the body's cells can use the carbohydrate glucose for energy, and the brain relies on glucose as its only fuel in normal situations. (It will use ketones for energy in the absence of glucose.) When eaten in excess, carbohydrates are stored in the muscles and the liver as glycogen. When these storage areas are full, any leftovers are converted to fat. The main dietary sources of carbohydrates in a Paleo diet are starchy vegetables, roots and tubers; fruits; all other vegetables; and to a lesser degree, nuts.

PROTEIN

This macronutrient is essential in building, maintaining and repairing the body's tissues. Protein is especially important for active folks whose muscles are continually being broken down during exercise. Adequate protein is crucial in muscle repair and recovery but that's not all they do! It's also a major constituent of many hormones and enzymes, plays a key role in immune function and can be used for energy in the absence of carbohydrates. Paleo sources of protein include all meats, poultry and eggs.

FATS

Contrary to what the fat-free and low-fat fad followers lead us to believe, fat is important and eating it is a good thing! Fat is necessary for normal growth and development, organ cushioning, fat-soluble vitamin absorption (vitamins A, D, E and K), energy (it's the most concentrated energy source) and for taste and satiation. There are some fats that are more beneficial than others though. The fat focus in the Paleo diet is on the most health-promoting types including coconut-sourced fats (oil, milk, meat); fat in grass-fed meats or lard rendered from the fat of grass-fed animals; olives and olive oil and a moderate amount of nuts.

WHAT ABOUT CHOLESTEROL?

Folks commonly associate the amount of cholesterol in foods (eggs, meat, butter and other tasty things) with blood cholesterol levels on lab reports. In fact, the cholesterol that we eat has little effect on our actual blood cholesterol levels. Only about 25 percent of the cholesterol in the body comes from food; the other 75 percent is made by the liver. Our bodies need cholesterol! It's part of every single cell, is needed for sex hormones (e.g., estrogen, testosterone) and bile-acid synthesis, and plays a key role in metabolizing the fat-soluble vitamins (A, D, E and K).

Since cholesterol is so important the body does a great job of regulating it. If your diet is high in cholesterol, your body makes less. If you eat a low-cholesterol diet, your body will make more to compensate.

YOU ATE WHAT? PALEO CONTROVERSIES

Everyone has an opinion, and no one's version of what is and isn't Paleo seems to match up with anyone else's. One person will make you walk the plank because you had a potato and the next person will tell you that rice and dairy are completely okay. What's the deal?

When evaluating if a food fits into your Paleo plan, you need to consider your health, lifestyle, tolerance and goals. If you are an athlete or a very active person who's healthy then potatoes and some occasional white rice may be totally fine for you. If you've got autoimmune or digestive issues or are trying to lose weight, those foods aren't going to be your best choices.

Dairy in and of itself is not Paleo. I'm fairly certain that the cave people weren't going out and milking the mammoths every morning so they could put cream in their coffee. The addition of dairy turns a Paleo diet into a Primal diet. Again, adding or not adding dairy needs to be an individual decision based on goals, health, lifestyle and tolerance. Whether or not they admit it, many people have a hard time digesting dairy. If getting lean is your goal, dairy isn't the best choice. If you're dealing with autoimmune or digestive issues, dairy should be avoided.

With all controversial foods it's a case of "different strokes for different folks." Consider your situation and find what works for you. There is no right or wrong answer that applies to everyone. You're navigating this Paleo journey and optimal health is the final destination!

Chapter 1

COOKING TIPS & TRICKS *for the* Paleo Foodie

For those of you new to cooking or new to Paleo, I've compiled some of my favorite kitchen tips and tricks! These are the tactics I use to keep costs down, cook efficiently and make meals that turn out delicious every time!

MONEY-SAVING TIPS

At first glance, real food seems expensive, especially compared to the abundance of cheap and unhealthy food available. This lifestyle does require us to spend more money per month on food than the average American, and committing to it may require that we make some shifts in our budgets. Although this isn't the cheapest way to eat, with a few tips and tricks, it can be made more affordable.

Ideally, I recommend that you make the recipes in this book using organic, pasture-raised and grass-fed ingredients. When cooking Paleo foods, we are using simple, fresh ingredients whose flavors, or lack thereof, won't be concealed with sugar- and salt-ridden packaged sauces. For this reason, the meals are only going to be as good as the ingredients used. Try to choose the best quality ingredients that you can afford.

If you can only afford the ingredients listed under "good" then that is perfectly fine. Start where your budget allows and I encourage you to make small changes as you learn more or as your budget increases.

DIFFERENT LEVELS OF FOOD QUALITY

FOOD ITEMS	GOOD	BETTER	BEST
Beef and Lamb	Antibiotic; no added hormones	Organic	100% Grass-fed and Finished
Poultry	Antibiotic Free	Organic	Pasture-raised
Pork	Antibiotic Free	Organic	Pasture-raised
Seafood	Sustainably Farmed	Wild Caught	Wild-caught and Sustainable
Dairy	Organic	Grass-fed	Grass-fed and Raw
Vegetables and Fruit	Conventional (stick to low pesticide options)	Organic	Organic and Local
Nuts	Organic	Organic and Raw*	Soaked and Dehydrated*
Eggs	Fed antibiotic free diet	Organic	Pasture-raised from local farms
Olive Oil			Organic, Extra-Virgin, unrefined, cold-pressed*
Coconut Oil		Organic, unrefined	Raw, organic, unrefined
Other Oils (i.e. Sesame, Macadamia)		Unrefined, cold or expeller pressed	Organic, unrefined, cold or expeller pressed

*Nuts: Since 2007, the USDA requires that growers sterilize almonds, even those labeled as "raw." This is done by heating them with steam, irradiating them, roasting or blanching, or treating them with propylene oxide (PPO). PPO is classified by the U.S. Environmental Protection Agency (EPA) as a probable human carcinogen. Choose organic almonds to avoid this chemical. To purchase truly raw almonds, they must be imported. You may also be able to find raw almonds at the farmers' market.

*Soaked and Dehydrated—Soaking and then dehydrating nuts reduces the phytic acid content and makes them more digestible.

*Imported olive oil is one of the most adulterated foods, often being cut with cheap, unhealthy oils like soybean oil. To avoid this, choose local olive oil or purchase from a trusted source, whenever possible.

CHOOSE TOUGH BUT FLAVORFUL CUTS OF MEAT

Eating like a foodie used to mean white-cloth dining and overpriced steaks. If you frequent farm-to-table restaurants, the traditional filet mignon is often missing, replaced by delicious, slow-braised meats and high-end versions of traditional comfort foods. Chuck roast is one of my favorite tough cuts of meat. For the best flavor, look for a roast that has thin ribbons of fat marbled throughout the beef, as this is where much of the flavor comes from.

BUY PROTEIN IN BULK, DIRECTLY FROM A RANCHER

Many people are discouraged from purchasing grass-fed beef due to the higher cost. Purchasing directly from a farmer or through a Community Supported Agriculture (CSA) program that offers meat is a great way to avoid paying this premium. An analysis published in the April 2011 issue of *Cooking Light* found the cost of grass-fed beef purchased directly from a farmer was only slightly higher than that of conventional beef. "Our cost per pound of Boutwell's beef was $5.32, including everything from ground beef to liver to filet mignon, which made it only marginally higher than similar quantities of regular grain-fed beef prices in local supermarkets." In addition, it is very satisfying knowing and trusting the person who produces your food.

JOIN A CSA

CSAs require members to pay at the onset of the growing season. Once harvesting begins, they will receive a weekly share of vegetables and fruit based on what is available. The vegetables and fruit are often harvested the day before, which is quite a treat in terms of flavor. CSAs are also very affordable. In our area, a small share is about $22 a week. We cook almost every night and struggle to get through our entire box. With a CSA, you won't know what you are receiving until that week, but it is a delightful surprise to open up your box of vegetables and anticipate your experiments for the week. CSAs also encourage you to try new ingredients!

SHOP AT YOUR LOCAL FARMERS' MARKET AND BUY FOODS THAT ARE IN SEASON

Foods are more expensive when they are out of season, and lack significant flavor. Choose recipes and ingredients that align with the season. Often farmers' markets are more affordable than health food stores, as the middleman is cut out, allowing the farmer to sell directly at a lower price.

PURCHASE SPICES AND DRIED HERBS FROM THE BULK SECTION

Spices and herbs sold in bulk bins are usually significantly cheaper than packaged spices and herbs. You can buy a small amount if that is all you need. Often, the more exotic herbs and spices are only found in the bulk bins. Spices don't tend to go bad, but with time become less potent. If you buy spices in smaller portions and replace them frequently, you will get the most in terms of flavor and freshness. Lastly, it is more environmentally friendly to buy in bulk, as it requires less packaging; you can also just bring your own packaging.

GROW AN HERB GARDEN

Many of my longtime blog readers (www.rubiesandradishes.com) know that I am a complete novice in the garden, but I see great value in growing herbs, even if you are inexperienced. Recipes usually call for a sprig of this or a teaspoon of that. Buying the entire bunch just to use a sprig adds immensely to the total cost of your recipe. Fresh-snipped herbs also tend to be more aromatic and flavorful. Rosemary, mint and thyme are a few examples of easy-to-grow herbs.

RELAX AND GET CREATIVE!

After you have made a recipe once and are familiar with the intended flavor, experiment with swapping out recipe ingredients for what you already have on hand. If a recipe calls for pistachios and you only have macadamia nuts, give them a try!

SETTING UP YOUR STATION

After working in restaurants as a server for several years and observing the chefs and cooks, the most valuable lesson I learned was to set up my station, or mise en place. Restaurants could not crank out quality food in a timely manner without a well-ordered, well-prepared kitchen. When I implemented this method at home, cooking became more relaxing and I started enjoying the process from start to finish. Prep cooking is now the part I look forward to the most!

You will have to find what works best for you, but in addition to my knife and cutting board, these are the components of my station:

- **INGREDIENT CONTAINER.** I recommend gathering all of your ingredients before you start cooking. I use one large, stainless steel bowl to gather all of my ingredients in.

- **GARBAGE OR COMPOST PAIL.** I use a second empty bowl for all my vegetable peelings and trimmings, which I save to compost. This tool has become as essential to me as my knives. Having a place to put your garbage will help you keep your prep space clean and clear, and will become the difference between being a frantic cook and a relaxed cook.

- **RAMEKINS.** I use small ramekins or containers for my chopped vegetables and spices. Since they may be needed at separate times, it is helpful to have them in individual containers. For efficiency, read through the recipe and use one container for ingredients that are added at the same time.

- **KITCHEN TOWEL.** To keep your work space clean.

Put on your favorite music, gather your ingredients and get chopping!

A FEW TIPS THAT CAN MAKE AN EDIBLE MEAL INTO A DELECTABLE MEAL!

- **TASTE AS YOU GO!** Recipe results can vary depending on your ingredients, your stove and even your altitude. Tasting as you go is the best way to ensure a delicious meal.

- **READ THE ENTIRE RECIPE BEFORE YOU START.** This will give you a chance to get familiar with the instructions and make sure you have everything you need.

- **DON'T RUSH.** Many of the recipes in this book require low and slow cooking, which allows the meat to become tender. Cooking at a higher heat for a shorter period will likely leave you with a tough, dry dish.

- **GET TO KNOW YOUR OVEN.** Many ovens don't cook at the intended temperature; they may run warmer or cooler. You can use an oven thermometer to check and adjust recipes accordingly.

- **BRING MEAT TO ROOM TEMPERATURE BEFORE COOKING.** Meats cook more evenly if started at room temperature. Smaller cuts of meat might only require 10 minutes of sitting before cooking. Larger cuts such as roasts might require 30 minutes.

Chapter 2

FATS & OILS

Fats are an essential component of cooking. They add flavor and texture to foods. They also are important to our health. They deliver the fat-soluble vitamins A, D, E and K throughout our bodies. In addition, fat plays a major role in helping us feel satiated and full. Basically, fat is where it's at!

FOR THE LOVE OF BUTTER

To say that I love butter would be an understatement. When I was growing up, I used it in my egg salad instead of mayonnaise. When I was pregnant, I ate it by the spoonful.

In the strictest sense, butter is not Paleo, as no dairy was consumed in the Paleolithic era. As the Paleo movement has evolved, butter and ghee have become much-accepted and even praised foods by those who tolerate them. Butter from grass-fed or pasture-raised cows is a nutritional powerhouse.

Butter is a rich source of fat-soluble vitamins A, D, E and K. Vitamin A, in particular, is essential to a healthy immune system. Butter is also a good source of vitamin K-2, which has been found to help protect us from heart disease, promotes brain function and helps prevent cancer.

Once milk is removed, butter is left with very minimal traces of lactose and casein, the components some people are intolerant to. When milk solids are separated and removed, we are left with clarified butter or ghee, which have even less casein and lactose than butter. Clarified butter essentially is pure butter fat. It has a better tolerance to heat than butter, so is ideal for high-heat cooking.

Unless you're dealing with autoimmune issues or are intolerant, butter is a superfood and can and should be consumed generously.

For a foodie, nothing compares to butter's rich, creamy flavor. Butter adds complexity and flavor to sautéed vegetables, sauces and browned meats that cannot be achieved with nonanimal sources of fat.

I believe butter to be a true health food. The recipes in this book liberally use butter. If you are sensitive to butter and ghee, or you choose not to use them, refer to my guide for using fats and oils on page 24 to find a substitute.

WHY FAT IS ESSENTIAL TO OUR HEALTH

Low fat, fat free, reduced fat—the food industry leads us to believe that food products with these labels are healthy. They tell us fat is bad and blame everything from heart disease to cancer on fat. But what they're not telling us is that we need fat in order to live! It is an essential nutrient. Without it none of us would be alive.

Dietary fat is our precious source of the essential Omega 3 and Omega 6 fatty acids, which occur in nature in several different forms. The Omega 3 and 6 fats in plants, called Alpha Linolenic and Linoleic acid respectively, are transformed in the bodies of the animals we eat (and to a lesser degree, in our bodies) into the forms humans most need: DHA, the end-usable form of Omega 3, which is found in fish and grass-fed meats, and Arachidonic Acid, the form of Omega 6 that is found in organ meats and egg yolks. These fats are critical for bile flow, blood clotting, brain health, cell structure, temperature regulation, and for mediating inflammation. Our bodies need both Omega 3 and Omega 6 fats, in proper proportion to one another.

Fat is also where the body stores extra energy. When there is no food available, the body draws on fat stores to keep it running like a well-oiled machine. During exercise fat steps in as muscle fuel when glycogen stores have been depleted. (Note: This only happens after prolonged, strenuous exercise.) As a vital component of breast milk, fat is extremely important for optimal infant brain development. Additionally, this fabulous nutrient plays a key role in the brain, nervous system, skin and every cell in the body. Fat is mandatory for the absorption of the fat-soluble vitamins A, D, E and K and for hormone production.

Make healthy fats part of your daily meal plan and know that fat free is not the answer regardless of the hype.

FATS AND OILS SAFE FOR FRYING, SAUTÉING AND BROWNING

Saturated fats are the best options for cooking; since they are chemically stable, they are resistant to damage from heat. Opt for grass-fed, organic and unrefined options.

SATURATED ANIMAL FATS	NONANIMAL SATURATED FATS
Butter	Coconut Oil
Ghee or Clarified Butter	Palm Oil
Lard (Pork Fat)	
Duck Fat	
Tallow (Beef Fat)	
Schmaltz (Chicken or Goose Fat)	
Lamb Fat	
Goat Fat	

FATS AND OILS SAFE FOR COLD USE IN SALADS, SAUCES OR CONDIMENTS

These oils should be unrefined, expeller-pressed or cold-pressed to avoid high heat and chemical processing that will damage the oils.

FATS AND OILS SAFE FOR COLD USE	
Olive Oil	Nut Oils (e.g., Macadamia, Walnut)
Avocado oil	Seed Oils (e.g., Sesame, Flax, Hemp, Pumpkin)

UNHEALTHY FATS AND OILS TO AVOID

These fats are either man-made or highly processed with chemicals. These oils oxidize easily and become rancid, causing inflammation in the body. Avoid anything that is hydrogenated or partially hydrogenated.

FATS AND OILS TO AVOID	
Margarine or other butter substitutes	Sunflower Oil
Vegetable Oil	Rice bran Oil
Canola Oil	Grapeseed Oil
Corn Oil	Soybean Oil
Cottonseed Oil	Vegetable Shortening
Safflower Oil	

Chapter 3

Tasty TIDBITS

The appetizer is often my favorite part of a meal. I love being able to taste small bites of many different flavors. Appetizers also represent the beginning of the evening, and the excitement and anticipation of good food and great company to come.

In my experience, a well-executed cocktail hour provides an intimate atmosphere full of lively conversations. It feels less formal than dinner and allows guests to unwind, enjoy great food and catch up.

When I am the host I thoroughly enjoy overhearing the cheerful banter among my guests, while I finish the meal in the kitchen.

In this section, you will find some of my very favorite appetizers, including Paleo versions of some family recipes. These tidbits are not only tasty, but are also nourishing!

CREAMY BACON-WRAPPED DATES

SERVES 10 (2 PER PERSON)

I usually prep these, stage them in the oven and turn the oven on as soon as the first dinner guests arrive. Greeting guests with warm, gooey cashew cream, crunchy bacon and sweet dates always impresses them. These are usually gone within minutes!

INGREDIENTS

FOR THE FILLING:

1 cup/110 g raw, whole cashews

filtered water for soaking

⅓ cup/80 ml water

1 heaping tbsp/20 g of nutritional yeast from non-GMO beets

2 tbsp/6 g chives, chopped

6 large basil leaves, chopped

¼ cup/10 g fresh parsley

1 clove garlic

1 tbsp/15 ml fresh lemon juice

¼ tsp lemon zest

¼ tsp pepper

½ tsp sea salt

10 pieces of bacon, cut in half

20 Medjool dates, slit, seeds removed

COOKING INSTRUCTIONS

Place the cashews in a bowl and cover them with filtered water. Allow them to soak for 5 to 6 hours. Preheat oven to 400°F/204°C. Remove the cashews from the water, rinse them and place them in a food processor. Add ⅓ cup/ 80 ml filtered water and pulse until cashews are creamy, about 2 minutes. Add the rest of the filling ingredients (yeast, chives, basil, parsley, garlic, lemon juice, lemon zest, pepper) and pulse until they are well combined, about 1 more minute. Adjust salt to taste. Fill dates with cashew filling. Securely wrap each date in a half-piece of bacon. Arrange dates on a wire rack and set on a baking sheet. Bake for 15 minutes or until bacon is cooked through. Serve warm.

PANCETTA-WRAPPED FIGS WITH WALNUTS

SERVES 12 (2 PER PERSON)

Figs are harvested twice a year in California, in early summer and late summer or early fall. I always grab a basket or two as soon as I see them at the market. In my opinion, not many other fruits can compete with the sweet flavor and the soft texture of a fresh, ripe fig. Crunchy walnuts and savory pancetta provide the perfect accompaniment to this honeyed fruit.

INGREDIENTS

24 walnut pieces

12 large black mission figs, sliced in half

24 strips of pancetta, very thinly sliced

FOR THE VINAIGRETTE:

2 tsp/10 ml extra-virgin olive oil

2 tsp/10 ml balsamic vinegar

1 tsp/5 ml champagne vinegar

2 tsp/1 g mint, chopped

1 tsp/1 g chives, chopped

sea salt and pepper to taste

COOKING INSTRUCTIONS

Preheat oven to 350°F/177°C. Chop walnuts and press into the center of each fig. Wrap a piece of pancetta around the fig. Place figs on a baking sheet and cook for 30 minutes or until pancetta is browned. While they cook, stir the vinaigrette ingredients. Add salt and pepper to taste. Arrange figs on a platter and drizzle with vinaigrette.

PROSCIUTTO-WRAPPED MELON

SERVES 8

Prosciutto e melone is a classic Italian appetizer, perfect for a summer party. I chill my cantaloupe before making this dish to make it extra refreshing. The fresh ground black pepper adds the perfect amount of heat and complexity to this simple appetizer.

INGREDIENTS

4 cups/720 g ripe cantaloupe, chilled and cut into 2 inch/5 cm-long and 1 inch/2-cm wide pieces

10 mint leaves, julienned

½ tsp pepper

2 tbsp/30 ml champagne vinegar

4 oz/113 g thinly sliced prosciutto, torn into 1 inch/2-cm strips

COOKING INSTRUCTIONS

In a medium-sized bowl, combine the cantaloupe, mint leaves, black pepper and champagne vinegar. Wrap 1 piece of prosciutto around each piece of melon.

SMOKED SALMON NORI WRAPS WITH WASABI MAYO

SERVES 6

Iodine is a trace mineral that plays an essential role in optimal thyroid function. We should be conscious of iodine when following a Paleo diet. Many people may not be getting enough iodine when processed foods are eliminated and table salt is replaced by sea salt. Nori (dried seaweed pressed into thin sheets) is a great source of iodine. These rolls are a tasty way to include it in your diet. They are perfect as an appetizer, or in a larger portion for a light lunch.

INGREDIENTS

4 sheets of nori

8 pieces (4 oz/113 g) of smoked wild salmon

1 English cucumber, julienned

2 carrots, peeled and julienned

4 tbsp/55 g of Homemade Wasabi Mayonnaise (page 228)

COOKING INSTRUCTIONS

Place one sheet of nori on a flat surface. Place 2 pieces of salmon, some cucumber and carrot, and 1 tablespoon/14 g of wasabi mayo, about 2 inches/ 5 cm from the bottom edge.

Starting with the bottom edge, roll the nori around the fillings, pressing gently while you roll. The edges of the nori will stick together if slightly moistened; run warm water over your finger, then run your finger along the inside edge of the top flap. Press the moistened edge to the roll to seal. Repeat with the remaining rolls. Cut each roll into 6 pieces.

SPICY PARSNIP HUMMUS

SERVES 8

I wanted to make hummus similar to the kind that I enjoyed growing up. My mom's version uses a lot of garlic. I stayed mostly true to her recipe but slightly enhanced it by adding a little kick! I had her test it and she said the flavors were unbelievably close. I often serve hummus with sliced cucumber.

INGREDIENTS

2 cups/400 g parsnips, cooked

½ cup/75 g organic tahini

3 tbsp/45 ml lemon juice

4 cloves garlic

½ tsp sea salt

2 tbsp/30 ml extra-virgin olive oil

1 tsp/20 g crushed red pepper flakes

paprika (garnish)

COOKING INSTRUCTIONS

Bring a large pot of salted water to a boil. Add the parsnips and boil until soft, about 15 minutes. Drain the parsnips and place them into the food processor. Add the tahini, lemon juice, garlic, salt, olive oil and red pepper flakes. Purée until smooth. Taste and adjust salt accordingly. Sprinkle with a pinch of paprika for garnish.

IKRA, OR POOR MAN'S CAVIAR (MIDDLE EASTERN EGGPLANT SPREAD)

SERVES 12

When most of us think of a Middle Eastern eggplant appetizer, baba ghanoush comes to mind. Although it's a fantastic dip, my favorite Middle Eastern eggplant dish is the lesser-known ikra. The recipe for ikra varies from household to household, and even within a household! My dad grills the vegetables for this dish, while my mom broils them. I am a novice on the barbecue, so I usually prepare this my mom's way. I love the smoky flavors complemented by subtle sweetness from the tomatoes. Traditionally ikra is served with pita bread, but I often eat it by itself or with sliced cucumbers.

INGREDIENTS

3 medium eggplants

1 green bell pepper

1–2 serrano peppers

6 tomatoes, deep red and flavorful

½ medium onion

5 cloves garlic

2 tbsp/30 ml extra-virgin olive oil

2 tbsp/30 ml fresh lemon juice

1 tsp/5 g sea salt

½ tsp pepper

COOKING INSTRUCTIONS

Preheat oven to 350°F/177°C. Pierce each eggplant in several places with a fork and place on a baking sheet. Roast in the oven until soft (about 1 hour), turning over once. Allow eggplant to cool. Once cooled cut it in half lengthwise. Scoop out the flesh and place it in a medium-sized bowl. Discard the peel. Change oven setting to broil. Place peppers, tomatoes and onion under the broiler for 20 minutes, turning once halfway through. Allow to cool. Peel the skin from the tomatoes and peppers. In a food processor mix eggplant, tomatoes, peppers, onion and garlic. Transfer to a medium-sized bowl. Add olive oil, lemon juice, salt and pepper. Adjust salt and pepper to taste. Refrigerate for 3 hours to allow spread to cool and flavors to meld.

BABA GHANOUSH (MIDDLE EASTERN EGGPLANT DIP)

SERVES 8

Baba ghanoush offers a brilliant balance of flavor and texture. It is simultaneously light and creamy, and the roasted eggplant offers a hint of smoke. The tahini adds depth and body, while the olive oil lends a fruity finish.

As you make this dish several times, experiment with adjusting ingredients like tahini and lemon juice to your liking.

INGREDIENTS

2 medium eggplants

½ cup/75 g organic tahini

3 cloves garlic

¼ cup/60 ml extra virgin olive oil

2 tbsp/30 ml fresh lemon juice

½ tsp sea salt

¼ tsp cumin

⅛ tsp cayenne

1 tbsp/3 g fresh parsley, minced (garnish)

¼ tsp paprika (garnish)

COOKING INSTRUCTIONS

Preheat oven to 350°F/177°C. Pierce each eggplant in several places with a fork and place on a baking sheet. Roast in the oven until soft (about 1 hour), turning over once. Allow eggplant to cool. Once cooled cut in half lengthwise. Scoop out the flesh and place in a medium-sized bowl. Discard the peel. Add the remaining ingredients (tahini, garlic, olive oil, lemon juice, salt, cumin and cayenne) except parsley and paprika to the same bowl. Use a fork to mash together and mix until well combined. Garnish with parsley and paprika.

SARDINE SPREAD

SERVES 6

I rarely use canned products but fresh sardines are hard to come by. Sardines are loaded with nutrients, so it is worth the trade-off! They are a great source of omega-3 fats, vitamin D, vitamin B12 and selenium. If you do find fresh sardines, they taste delicious grilled!

INGREDIENTS

1 tbsp/15 g ghee

½ sweet onion, chopped

1 clove garlic, minced

8 oz/227 g of canned sardines, drained and mashed

½ cup/115 g avocado (about 1 medium avocado)

3 tbsp/44 ml fresh lemon juice

½ tsp lemon zest

¼ tsp cayenne pepper

cucumber slices for dipping

COOKING INSTRUCTIONS

Heat ghee in a saucepan over medium heat. Sauté onions until soft, about 7 minutes. Add garlic and sauté until fragrant, about 2 minutes. Place onions, garlic, sardines, avocado, lemon juice, lemon zest and cayenne pepper in a food processor and blend until smooth. Serve with cucumber slices for dipping.

FRIED PADRÓN PEPPERS

SERVES 4

Pimientos de Padrón are small green peppers from the Galicia region of Spain. I first learned about Padrón peppers while strolling through the farmers' market with a girlfriend who frequents Spain. She told me they were delicious fried with olive oil and sprinkled with sea salt. She was absolutely right! Since olive oil is not ideal for high-heat cooking, I experimented with alternative fats to use for this recipe. I have found that the neutral flavor of duck fat best complements the slightly sweet and mild flavor of these peppers.

INGREDIENTS

1 tbsp/15 ml duck fat

25-30 Padrón peppers

sea salt

COOKING INSTRUCTIONS

Heat a heavy skillet, preferably cast iron, over medium heat. Add the duck fat to the skillet. Once it has liquefied add the peppers, turning until they are well coated with the oil and blistered, about 4 to 5 minutes. Transfer to a plate and sprinkle with sea salt.

GRILLED LAMB HEARTS AND LIVER WITH SPICY CHIMICHURRI

SERVES 6 TO 8

Liver is rich in iron and other minerals, choline and B vitamins, especially vitamins B6 and B12. In addition, it's a good source of the fat-soluble vitamins A, D and K. Heart is a rich source of Coenzyme Q10 and a helpful substance that supports many body processes.

In Armenian cuisine organ meats are often served simply, grilled and sprinkled with sea salt. Because of its milder flavor, lamb offal is preferred over beef.

Heart is a perfect introduction to organ meats. Once it's trimmed, you're left with tender muscle flesh, which resembles other muscle meats in flavor.

Liver and heart are quite lean. I add a sauce to the classic grilled version to add some fat to the dish. Let's face it; it will also help disguise the strong flavor of liver for those who are new to it!

INGREDIENTS

1 lb/454 g lamb heart, well-trimmed of exterior fat and interior veins and ventricles, cut into 1 inch/2-cm cubes

1 lb/454 g lamb liver, trimmed of tough membranes and veins, cut into 2 inch/5-cm slices

coarse sea salt

Serve with Four-Herb Spicy Chimichurri (page 211)

COOKING INSTRUCTIONS

Thread the heart and liver slices loosely on skewers and sprinkle with sea salt. Grill medium over hot coals, about 5 minutes per side, until the center is pink but firm. Do not overcook, as the heart and liver can get really tough. Drizzle with chimichurri and serve.

SALMON CEVICHE WITH MANGO AND CUCUMBER

SERVES 4

Ceviche is a Latin American preparation using citrus acid to "cook" fish. Because this dish isn't cooked with heat, use the freshest fish possible. During salmon season, we often make ceviche with fish we buy directly from fishermen off their boats—a real treat!

INGREDIENTS

1 lb/454 g salmon fillet, skin removed, diced

1 serrano pepper, minced

3 tbsp/10 g scallions, chopped

1 mango, peeled and diced

½ cup/90 g cucumber, peeled and chopped

¼ cup/10 g cilantro, finely chopped

1 tbsp/3 g mint leaves, chopped

¼ cup/60 ml each fresh lemon, lime and orange juice

¼ tsp sea salt

¼ tsp pepper

1 avocado, chopped

COOKING INSTRUCTIONS

In a medium-sized bowl combine salmon, serrano pepper, scallions, mango, cucumber, cilantro and mint. Add lemon, lime and orange juices, salt and pepper and make sure all of the ingredients are well coated. Place in the refrigerator for 1 to 2 hours. Fold in avocado, taking care not to smash. Adjust salt and pepper to taste and serve.

COCONUT SHRIMP WITH MANGO SALSA

SERVES 4

I worked as a server at a restaurant through graduate school. Coconut shrimp was one of my favorite appetizers. Of course, the version I consumed at the restaurant I worked at was loaded with vegetable oils and doused in white flour. What I love about the Paleo diet is that I can enjoy my old favorite foods without the guilty conscience. My old favorites are improved with their Paleo face-lifts!

INGREDIENTS

½ cup/50 g coconut flour

2 tbsp/15 g arrowroot starch

½ tsp cayenne

½ tsp sea salt

2 eggs, lightly beaten

1 cup/75 g dried shredded coconut

1 lb/455 g fresh shrimp, shelled and deveined

½ cup/120 ml coconut oil for frying

Serve with Mango Salsa (page 220)

COOKING INSTRUCTIONS

In a medium-sized bowl mix together coconut flour, arrowroot starch, cayenne and salt. Place the beaten eggs in a second bowl. Place the shredded coconut in a third bowl. Hold the tail of each shrimp and dip it in the egg mixture, making sure both sides are covered. Dip each shrimp in the coconut flour mixture, then back into the egg mixture. Once the shrimp is coated with egg a second time, dip it into the shredded coconut. Make sure it is well coated with coconut. Place a heavy-bottomed skillet on medium-low heat and add the coconut oil. Once the coconut oil has melted add the shrimp to the skillet. Cook shrimp for about 5 minutes on the first side, and an additional 2 to 3 minutes on the second side. (It works best to cook these a bit longer on a lower heat so the coconut does not burn.) Serve with mango salsa.

SHRIMP WITH PAPAYA COCKTAIL SAUCE

SERVES 8

Although I love shrimp, I have never been a fan of restaurant shrimp with cocktail sauce. Too often the shrimp is served with prepackaged, too-sweet, ketchup-tasting sauce. This papaya version is a fruity and refreshing take on an old classic.

INGREDIENTS

FOR THE COCKTAIL SAUCE:

1 medium papaya, diced (about 2 cups/480 g)

2 tsp/40 g freshly grated horseradish

1 tbsp/15 ml champagne vinegar

2 tbsp/30 ml fresh lime juice

1 tsp/5 ml raw honey

1 serrano pepper, chopped

½ tsp sea salt

FOR THE SHRIMP:

zest of 1 lemon

¼ cup/60 ml fresh lemon juice

1 tbsp/15 ml sea salt

1 bay leaf

3 qts/2.8 L water

2 lbs/900 g large shrimp, peeled and deveined

COOKING INSTRUCTIONS

Prepare the cocktail sauce by placing all of the ingredients (papaya, horseradish, vinegar, lime juice, honey, pepper, salt) in a food processor. Pulse a few times until well combined. Do not grate the horseradish too far in advance, since within a few hours it can turn drab and bitter.

Prepare the shrimp by adding lemon zest, lemon juice, salt and the bay leaf to 3 quarts/2.8 liters of water. Bring to a boil, then reduce to a simmer. Add the shrimp and poach until opaque, about 3 to 4 minutes. Serve shrimp along with papaya cocktail sauce.

CHEF'S TIP
Choose organic papayas; nonorganic papayas are sometimes genetically modified.

SWEET POTATO SALMON CAKES

SERVES 4 (3 PER PERSON)

Salmon is often revered for its high omega-3 fat content, and is also a great source of vitamin B12, tryptohan, selenium and vitamin D (which is not found in many foods).

I often use canned salmon in this recipe because the salmon flavor is not as prominent when combined with the rest of the ingredients. Buying canned salmon offers a great opportunity for a Paleo foodie to save money. Reserve the fresh salmon for a recipe where it's the star.

INGREDIENTS

¼ cup/10 g parsley, chopped

¼ cup/10 g scallions, chopped

¼ cup/45 g red bell pepper, chopped

12 oz/340 g of canned, boneless pink salmon or cooked fresh salmon

1 medium sweet potato, peeled, boiled and mashed

2 eggs, separated

¼ tsp cayenne pepper

½ tsp sea salt

¼ tsp pepper

2 tbsp/30 ml coconut milk (see page 207 for Homemade Coconut Milk)

2 tbsp/15 g coconut flour

2 tbsp/15 g arrowroot starch

¼ cup/60 ml coconut oil for frying

COOKING INSTRUCTIONS

In the bowl of a food processor combine parsley, scallions and red bell pepper. Pulse a few times until well combined. In a medium bowl, combine the parsley, scallion and red bell pepper mixture, salmon, sweet potato, egg yolks, cayenne, sea salt, black pepper, coconut milk, coconut flour and arrowroot starch. Mix using your hands, until all the ingredients are well combined.

Make the mixture into patties, about the size of your palm and 1-inch/2.5-cm thick. This mixture should make about 12 patties. Heat a heavy-bottomed skillet, such as cast iron, over medium heat. Add coconut oil. Using a pastry brush, coat both sides of each patty with egg whites. Once coconut oil is melted, add the salmon cakes to the pan and cook for 3 to 5 minutes per side. Cook in batches so as not to overcrowd the pan. Add more coconut oil as needed. Cook until well browned, crispy and heated through.

SPICY SAUSAGE- AND WALNUT-STUFFED MUSHROOMS

SERVES 6

One-bite appetizers give parties a more intimate feel, making room for lively conversation. I recently shared these savory treats with my book club. (If you saw our spread, you might call it a wine and food club!) The fiery sausage pairs perfectly with the earthy mushrooms, making this appetizer an instant crowd-pleaser!

INGREDIENTS

18-24 crimini mushrooms

1 tbsp/15 g ghee

½ lb/225 g spicy Italian sausages

¼ cup/60 g shallots, finely minced

2 cloves garlic, minced

¼ tsp fennel seeds

2 tbsp/15 g walnuts, chopped

¼ cup/10 g fresh parsley, chopped

sea salt and pepper to taste

1 tbsp/15 g butter, melted

COOKING INSTRUCTIONS

Preheat oven to 375°F/190°C. Pull the stems off the mushrooms and chop the stems, keeping the mushroom caps whole. Heat the ghee in a medium skillet over medium heat. Remove the sausage meat from the casings and crumble into the skillet. Sauté gently until meat is cooked through. Use a slotted spoon to remove the sausage, leaving the fat behind. Using the remaining sausage fat, sauté the shallots and mushroom stems until tender, about 5 to 7 minutes. Then add garlic, fennel seeds and walnuts and sauté until fragrant, about 1 to 2 minutes. Add parsley and the sausage mixture back in. Make sure the meat and mushroom mixture is thoroughly mixed. Adjust salt and pepper to taste. Toss mushroom caps with melted butter. Generously fill with stuffing. Place on a baking sheet and cook for 20 minutes or until well browned.

HOMEMADE NUT BARS

SERVES 8

These nut bars make a filling, sweet treat. If you will be hosting kids or toddlers as guests, these are always a hit!

INGREDIENTS

½ cup/85 g almonds

½ cup/60 g walnuts

13 dates, pits removed and chopped (a little more than a cup)

¾ cup/55 g shredded coconut

1 tbsp/15 ml coconut oil

½ tsp cinnamon

¼ tsp nutmeg

COOKING INSTRUCTIONS

Add the almonds and walnuts to a food processor and blend until you have a fine, flour texture. Next add the dates, shredded coconut, coconut oil, cinnamon and nutmeg. The coconut oil should be soft. If it is really hard, melt it before adding. Blend until the ingredients are well combined. The mixture should be slightly sticky. Put the mixture in a square or rectangular glass dish. Use the back of a spoon to push on it and pack it in tight. Place it in the refrigerator to set for at least an hour. Slice it into squares and serve or store in the refrigerator.

Chapter 4

FOOD LOVER'S
Fare

Following a Paleo diet restored my love of food and cooking. I started noticing Paleo recipes, or recipes that were very easy to convert, everywhere. I mostly noticed how many ethnic cuisines offered a variety of dishes that were inherently Paleo, including traditional Persian and Armenian dishes. I was motivated to learn how to make some of my family's favorite dishes. Many of these are Middle Eastern dishes, with distinct flavors and involved cooking methods.

When I was growing up, turmeric and saffron were the most-used spices in my house. Turmeric adds a slight earthy and pungent flavor to dishes. Saffron has a very unique flavor and an exotic aroma. Saffron adds an earthy and floral richness to dishes. A little of each of these spices can go a long way; too much can overwhelm a dish instead of pleasantly elevating it. If you are new to ethnic cooking, I hope you give some of these unique dishes a try. They are always a hit with my American friends.

Like most Paleo families, we enjoy our fair share of protein. We eat it all and are always excited to try something new. Many of the recipes I have included here call for slow braising in the oven or on the stovetop. Although these methods require a little more time and attention, you are rewarded with succulent, tender and flavorful meat. These methods also allow you to use inexpensive yet flavorful cuts of meat to turn them into sophisticated fare.

BANGKOK MEATBALLS

SERVES 6

This twist on a traditional meatball is to die for! Thai flavors are some of my favorites and I jump at every opportunity to experiment with them.

Thai chili peppers are sometimes hard to come by. If you can't find some, serrano peppers make a good substitute.

INGREDIENTS

4 scallions, chopped

1 inch/2 cm fresh ginger, peeled and chopped

1 stalk lemongrass (the pale yellow parts only), chopped

1 tbsp/15 g fish sauce

1 tbsp/15 ml fresh lime juice

6 Thai basil leaves

2 Thai chili peppers, chopped

2 lbs/910 g ground turkey

2 tsp/15 g raw honey

2 eggs, lightly whisked

1 tsp/5 g sea salt

½ tsp pepper

1 tbsp/2 g arrowroot starch

coconut oil for frying

COOKING INSTRUCTIONS

Place scallions, ginger, lemongrass, fish sauce, lime juice, basil leaves and chili peppers in a food processor until the mixture forms a paste. Add it to the meat and combine, but do not overmix. Whisk the honey into the eggs. Add the egg and honey mixture to the meat. Add salt and pepper. Sprinkle the mixture with arrowroot; fold it in until it disappears. Using a tablespoon, scoop up some of the meatball mixture and shape it into a ball. Heat a wok over medium heat. Add enough coconut oil to cover half of the meatballs. Drop the meatballs into the wok to fry. Using a spoon, turn the meatballs to fry the other side. Cook until the meatballs are browned on all sides, about 10 minutes. Move to a plate lined with paper towels to drain.

CHEF'S TIP
If you don't have a wok, place ¼ cup/60 ml coconut oil in a skillet. Keep turning your meatballs until they are browned on all sides.

PALEO KOOFTEH (PERSIAN MEATBALLS)

SERVES 4 (MAKES 10 MEATBALLS)

Like most Middle Eastern dishes, koofteh takes a while to make because the meatballs are simmered in broth, low and slow. This dish is perfect for a leisurely weekend dinner. Traditionally this recipe calls for white rice, but I've substituted cauliflower rice, which works surprisingly well! No one in my family has ever even noticed the missing rice.

INGREDIENTS

2 strands of saffron

2 tsp/10 ml of filtered water

FOR THE FILLING:

1 tbsp/15 g ghee

½ onion, diced

½ cup/60 g walnuts, chopped

½ cup/85 g prunes, chopped

FOR THE SAUCE:

1 tbsp/15 g ghee

½ onion, diced

2 cloves garlic, crushed

½ tsp turmeric

6 tomatoes, peeled, chopped and seeds removed

2 cups/475 ml filtered water

½ tsp sea salt

FOR THE MEATBALLS:

1 cup/230 ml cauliflower

½ tsp sea salt

¼ tsp pepper

1 lb/455 g ground beef

½ onion, grated

1 egg

½ cup/20 g fresh parsley, chopped

¼ cup/10 g mint, chopped

½ tsp turmeric

tomato broth

COOKING INSTRUCTIONS

Place the strands of saffron in a small bowl and cover with 2 teaspoons/10 ml of water and set aside. Prepare the filling. Heat a large sauté pan over medium heat, preferably one with a large, flat base and shallow sides. Add 1 tablespoon/ 15 g of ghee and sauté half the diced onion in ghee until translucent. Add the walnuts and prunes and sauté for a few minutes until well combined. Set the filling aside.

Prepare the sauce. Add another tablespoon/15 g of ghee to the same pan and sauté the remaining half onion until soft and translucent, about 10 minutes. Add garlic and turmeric. Stir well and sauté for 2 more minutes. Add chopped tomatoes, water and salt. Cover and simmer on low heat while you form the meatballs.

To form the meatballs, remove the stem of the cauliflower and put through food processor until it resembles rice. In a large bowl, combine cauliflower, salt, pepper, meat, grated onions, eggs, parsley, mint, turmeric and saffron and mix well. Round mixture into balls, poke a hole in the middle, fill with filling and close. You should be able to make about 10 meatballs.

Slowly place the meatballs in the simmering sauce. Cook on low heat for an hour or until meatballs are cooked through. Carefully turn the meatballs halfway through cooking so both sides have a chance to be immersed in the liquid. Serve meatballs in bowls along with tomato broth.

PALEO PERSIAN KOTLET (CUTLET)

SERVES 4

This was one of my favorite meals my mom made for us growing up. She often served the *kotlets* with homemade French fries. I have made a few minor Paleo adjustments to her original recipe: I have omitted white flour and swapped out the white potato for sweet potato. Although you can make kotlets with white potato, I think the sweet potato adds a note of complexity to this Middle Eastern comfort food.

Traditionally, these are served hot or cold. They are great to pack for a Paleo picnic.

INGREDIENTS

1 sweet potato, peeled and chopped (about 3 cups/710 ml)

½ large onion, chopped

3 garlic cloves

3 tbsp/8 g fresh parsley

1 lb/455 g ground beef

¼ tsp turmeric

½ tsp sea salt

¼ tsp pepper

1 egg

3 tbsp/45 g ghee, lard or duck fat for frying

Crispy Sage (page 213), tomatoes, pickles, olives (garnish)

COOKING INSTRUCTIONS

Place sweet potato, onion, garlic and parsley in a food processor. Pulse until well combined. If the mixture gives off any liquid, drain the liquid before combining it with the meat. Combine the mixture with the meat, turmeric, salt, pepper and egg. Mix until well combined.

Heat a heavy-bottomed skillet such as cast iron over medium heat. Add ghee or fat. Take a handful of the meat mixture and shape into a ball. Continue to flatten into an oval shape.

Place flattened kotlets into the skillet. This will have to be done in batches. Take care not to overcrowd the pan. Fry until both sides are well browned and cooked through, about 5 minutes per side. Add more fat as needed. Drain the kotlets on a paper-towel-lined plate. Serve with Crispy Sage, sliced tomatoes, pickles and olives.

FLANK STEAK WITH CILANTRO SAUCE

SERVES 8

I liberally use fresh herbs in my cooking, partly due to my background. Both Armenian and Persian cuisines are very herb heavy. One of my favorite ways to use fresh herbs is to make sauces to serve with grilled meats. This simple cilantro sauce adds a zesty freshness to this flavorful meat.

Flank Steak with Cilantro Sauce is a great option for summer entertaining. Serve it with my Whole Roasted Sweet Potatoes with Two Toppings (page 172) for a complete meal.

INGREDIENTS

FOR THE MARINADE:

2 tsp/10 g ground cumin

1 chili pepper, minced

½ cup/120 ml fresh lime juice

¼ cup/60 ml extra-virgin olive oil

1 tsp/5 g sea salt

½ tsp pepper

3 lbs/1 kg flank steak

FOR THE SAUCE (MAKES ½ CUP/118 ML):

2 medium garlic cloves

1 ½ cups/60 g cilantro

2 tbsp/20 g red bell pepper, chopped

¼ cup/60 ml extra-virgin olive oil

1 ½ tbsp/25 ml red wine vinegar

½ tsp chili powder

½ tsp sea salt

COOKING INSTRUCTIONS

Make the marinade by mixing together the cumin, chili pepper, lime juice, olive oil, salt and pepper. Pour over the flank steak. Make sure it is well coated. Cover and marinate for at least 4 hours, up to overnight.

Make the cilantro sauce by adding the garlic cloves, cilantro, red bell pepper, olive oil, red wine vinegar, chili powder and salt to the bowl of a food processor. Mix until combined but still slightly chunky. Take care to not liquefy the sauce too much. The sauce can be made ahead to allow flavors to further develop.

Preheat a grill to medium-high heat. Grill the steaks for about 6–8 minutes per side for medium. Grilling times will depend on the thickness of your flank steak. Thinner parts will cook quicker. Cut the steak against the grain and serve drizzled with cilantro sauce.

CHEF'S TIP

For even grilling, remove the steak from the marinade and allow it to come to room temperature about 30 minutes before grilling.

BEEF CHEEK BRAISED WITH TOMATOES

SERVES 6

Beef cheeks, called *joues de boeuf* in French, are an inexpensive and often overlooked cut of meat. As a result of the extensive chewing cows do, they are one of the toughest cuts of meat on the cow. When cooked properly, the connective tissue softens and the meat melts in your mouth. The result is a tender and heavenly piece of meat.

INGREDIENTS

2 beef cheeks

1 tsp/5 g sea salt

½ tsp pepper

½ tsp chili powder

2 tbsp/30 g ghee

1 white onion, diced

6 cloves garlic, minced

2 tbsp/30 ml tomato paste (preferably from a jar)

6 tomatoes, chopped, peeled and cored

2 cups/472 ml Beef Broth (page 204)

COOKING INSTRUCTIONS

Rub beef cheeks with salt, pepper and chili powder on both sides. Heat a heavy-bottomed skillet over medium heat. Add ghee to hot pan. Once ghee is hot, add the beef cheeks and brown on both sides, about 3 minutes per side. Set aside. Add the onion to the pan and sauté until soft, about 5 minutes, then add garlic and sauté until fragrant, about 1 minute. Add tomato paste and tomatoes and scrape the pan with a wooden spoon to get up any brown bits. Place browned beef cheeks in the slow cooker. Pour the tomato-onion mixture and beef broth over it. Cook on low heat for 8 hours.

SLOW-COOKER HORSERADISH AND PARSNIP POT ROAST

SERVES 8

The slow-cooking process tames the heat of the horseradish in this dish, but it still offers enough savory flavor to complement the sweetness of the parsnips.

INGREDIENTS

2 tbsp/30 g ghee

sea salt and pepper

3 lbs–4 lbs/1–2 kg beef chuck roast

1 onion, sliced

2 tbsp/10 ml tomato paste (preferably from a jar)

3 tbsp/30 g Horseradish (page 217)

6 cloves garlic, minced

¼ tsp paprika

½ cup/120 ml Beef Broth (page 204)

2 bay leaves

3 sprigs fresh thyme

2 carrots, peeled and chopped

4 large parsnips, cubed and chopped

COOKING INSTRUCTIONS

Heat a heavy-bottomed pan or cast-iron skillet on medium-high heat. Add the ghee. Generously salt and pepper the roast. When the ghee is warm, add the roast to the pan and brown on all sides, about 1 to 2 minutes per side. Set aside.

Add the onions to the pan and sauté until translucent, about 5 minutes. Add the tomato paste and cook until the color of the paste changes from a bright red to a brick color, about 1 minute. Transfer the onion mixture to the slow cooker.

In a small bowl combine the horseradish, garlic and paprika. Generously rub the mixture all over the roast. Place the roast in the slow cooker. Add broth, bay leaves, thyme, carrots and parsnips to the slow cooker. Turn to low and cook for 8 hours. Discard the sprigs of thyme and bay leaves. Serve roast with parsnips and carrots.

CHEF'S TIP
To avoid soggy vegetables, add the carrots and parsnips halfway through cooking time.

SAUTÉED BEEF OVER WATERCRESS

SERVES 6

Inspired by a delicious meal at a Vietnamese restaurant in New York City, this dish skips the oyster sauce but stays true to the notion of beef sautéed with lots of onions, garlic and scallions, and served over watercress. The sweetness of the well-cooked onions with the peppery watercress and the flavorful beef offer a tantalizing treat to the taste buds.

INGREDIENTS

FOR THE MARINADE:

¼ cup/60 ml coconut aminos

2 tbsp/30 ml fresh lime juice

2 tbsp/30 ml sesame oil (unrefined, expeller- or cold-pressed)

3 cloves garlic, minced

1 tbsp/20 g raw honey

1 tbsp/15 g fresh ginger, minced

2 tbsp/5 g green onions, chopped

1 tbsp/15 g fish sauce

1 ½ lbs/680 g flank steak

FOR THE DRESSING:

1 tbsp/15 ml fresh orange juice

1 tbsp/15 ml fresh lime juice

1 tbsp/15 ml coconut aminos

1 tsp/7 g raw honey

1 tbsp/15 ml sesame oil (unrefined, expeller- or cold-pressed)

¼ tsp red chili flakes

3 tbsp/45 ml expeller-pressed coconut oil

2 cups/260 g white onion, sliced

¾ cup/40 g scallions, chopped

4 large garlic cloves or 6 medium, minced

2 bunches watercress leaves

COOKING INSTRUCTIONS

Make the marinade by mixing together the coconut aminos, lime juice, sesame oil, garlic, honey, ginger, green onions and fish sauce. Pour over the flank steak. Make sure it is well coated. Cover and marinate for at least 4 hours, up to overnight. Flank steak can be tough, so the longer it marinates the more tender it will become.

Make the dressing by whisking together orange juice, lime juice, coconut aminos, honey, sesame oil and chili flakes. Set aside.

Heat a wok or a large, heavy-bottomed skillet to medium-high heat. Add the coconut oil. Once the oil is warm, add the beef and sauté until cooked through, about 6 to 8 minutes. Set beef aside. Add onions and sauté until translucent, about 7 minutes. Add scallions and garlic and sauté until scallions are soft, about 3 minutes. Add beef back in and sauté until beef is warm, about 2 minutes. Place a large handful of watercress on a plate, drizzle with 2 teaspoons/10 ml of dressing and top with warm beef and onion sauté.

CHEF'S TIP
I prefer using expeller-pressed coconut oil for this dish, as it does not have a strong coconut flavor.

PANFRIED FILET WITH SHALLOT SAUCE

SERVES 4

Most of us reserve indulging in an elegant filet mignon for a celebratory restaurant meal. That restaurant filet can easily be made at home, with higher quality ingredients and at a fraction of the price. Even fancy restaurants are likely going to use vegetable oil for searing their steaks. At home you can use grass-fed butter or another fat of your choice. Once you top your steak with this luscious shallot pan sauce, it will triumph over most of the steaks you have had at a restaurant.

INGREDIENTS

4 oz–6 oz/115–170 g beef filets

2 tbsp/30 ml unsalted butter, melted

FOR THE SAUCE:

2 tbsp/30 ml unsalted butter, melted

1 cup/240 g shallots, thinly sliced

sea salt and pepper

1 tbsp/15 ml red wine vinegar

½ cup/120 ml Beef Broth (page 204)

1 tbsp/2 g fresh rosemary, finely chopped

COOKING INSTRUCTIONS

Let the steaks come to room temperature, about 30 minutes. Preheat oven to 400°F/204°C. Place an oven-safe, glass baking dish in the oven to warm up. Heat a large cast-iron skillet on medium-high. Brush melted butter onto one side of the steak. When the skillet is ready, add the steaks. While the first side is browning, brush the other side with butter. Once a nice brown crust forms, about 2 to 3 minutes, use tongs to flip the steaks and sear the other side. Using tongs transfer steaks to the warm dish in the oven and roast for 6 to 8 minutes for medium-rare.

While the steaks are roasting, make your sauce. Add 1 tablespoon/15 ml of butter to the same cast-iron skillet used to brown the steaks. Add the shallots and season generously with salt and pepper. Continue to cook until the shallots are softened, about 10 minutes. Add the vinegar and cook until it evaporates. Add the broth and bring to a boil. Allow the sauce to cook until it has reduced by half. Pull the pan from the heat, stir in the remaining tablespoon of butter and rosemary. Remove steaks, salt and pepper and let rest for 5 minutes. Serve topped with shallot sauce.

OSSO BUCO

SERVES 6

There are many reasons to love osso buco, one being the delectable marrow in the center that adds a delicious richness to the sauce. What makes this dish for me, though, is the gremolata, a garnish typically made from chopped parsley, garlic and lemon zest. I love how the fresh flavors of the herbs brighten up a luscious meal.

Traditionally this dish is made with veal, but if you don't have access to humanely raised veal, then beef shanks will work, too!

INGREDIENTS

FOR THE GREMOLATA:

1 cup/40 g fresh flat-leaf parsley

2 tbsp/20 g pine nuts

2 small cloves garlic or 1 large clove

zest of 1 lemon

1 tbsp/15 ml fresh lemon juice

2 tbsp/30 ml extra-virgin olive oil

¼ tsp sea salt

¼ tsp pepper

2 lbs/900 g veal shanks or beef shanks

sea salt and pepper

3 tbsp/43 g ghee

1 large onion, chopped

4 cloves garlic, crushed

2 carrots, peeled and chopped

2 ribs celery, chopped

2 tbsp/30 ml tomato paste (preferably from a jar)

½ cup/120 ml white wine

1 cup/235 ml Beef Broth (page 204)

COOKING INSTRUCTIONS

To make the gremolata, combine all of the ingredients (parsley, pine nuts, garlic, lemon zest, lemon juice, olive oil) in a food processor and pulse until well combined but still chunky. Adjust salt and pepper to taste. Set aside.

Generously season the veal with salt and pepper. Melt the ghee in a heavy-bottomed pan or a Dutch oven over medium heat. Add the shanks and cook until browned on all sides. Set veal aside and add onion to the pan. Cook until onions are tender, about 10 minutes. Add garlic, carrots and celery and cook until fragrant, about 5 minutes. Add the tomato paste, then add wine and use a wooden spoon to scrape up any brown bits from the bottom of the pan. Add the shanks back to the pan, along with the beef broth. Cover and simmer over low heat for 1½ hours or until meat is tender, occasionally basting the shanks. To serve, arrange the shanks on dinner plates, spoon a generous amount of sauce from the pan over them, and sprinkle them with gremolata.

SUN-DRIED-TOMATO-AND-FENNEL-BRAISED SHORT RIBS

SERVES 4

Beef short ribs are packed with flavor and become unbelievably tender when slowly cooked. The sun-dried tomatoes and fennel give these braised short ribs a Mediterranean twist.

INGREDIENTS

2 ½ lbs/1 kg beef short ribs

2 tsp/10 g coriander

2 tsp/10 g cumin

sea salt and pepper

2 tbsp/30 g ghee

1 onion, sliced

1 medium fennel bulb, sliced

¼ cup/40 g green garlic, chopped

¼ cup/40 g sun-dried tomatoes, chopped

1 cup/235 ml dry red wine

3 cups/710 ml Beef Broth (page 204)

2 bay leaves

COOKING INSTRUCTIONS

Preheat oven to 350°F/177°C. Toss ribs with coriander and cumin, and generously salt and pepper. Heat a Dutch oven or heavy-bottomed, ovenproof pan on medium-high heat. Add the ghee to the pan. Once the ghee is hot, add the ribs and brown on all sides, about 3 minutes per side. Transfer to a plate and set aside.

Add the onion to the pan and sauté until translucent, about 5 minutes. Add the fennel, green garlic and sun-dried tomatoes and sauté until fragrant, about 2 to 3 minutes. Add the wine and scrape up any brown bits from the bottom of the pan. Add the broth and bay leaves and the ribs to the pan. Cover and transfer the pan to the oven. Cook for 1½ hours, basting and turning 1 or 2 times. Uncover and cook for an additional 45 minutes. Discard bay leaves before serving.

CHEF'S TIP
If you can't find green garlic, then substitute 4 cloves garlic, minced.

GRAPE LEAF AND CABBAGE DOLMAS

SERVES 10

Many Armenian dishes require long prep times and then cook "low and slow." I remember spending half a day making these with my mom and grandma! So we always made dolmas in bulk for a few meals. You can halve the recipe or freeze the leftovers for another night. Dolma is traditionally paired with plain, thick yogurt.

INGREDIENTS

1 bunch fresh cilantro

2 bunches fresh parsley

1 bunch scallions

1 bunch fresh dill

1 head cabbage, halved

1 jar grape leaves

2 lbs/900 g grass-fed ground beef

1 tbsp/15 g sea salt

1 tsp/5 g pepper

½ tsp cayenne

½ tsp turmeric

2 tbsp/30 g butter, softened (not needed if using conventional beef)

½ lemon

2 tbsp/30 ml tomato paste (preferably from a jar)

4 cups/950 ml of water, divided

COOKING INSTRUCTIONS

Wash and thoroughly dry your herbs. If they are wet, you will risk making the meat mixture soggy. Pulse the cilantro, parsley, scallions and dill in the food processor until well minced but not too smashed. Set aside.

Bring a pot of water to a boil and add the cabbage. Cook for 15 minutes, until soft. Strain in a colander.

Drain the grape leaves and separate them. Mix the meat, herb mixture, salt, pepper, cayenne and turmeric. Mix in butter only if using grass-fed beef; conventional beef has enough fat and won't need additional butter. Squeeze the half-lemon's juice into the mix. Use your hands to make sure the mixture is well combined.

Lay the grape leaves, vein side up, stem toward you. Place 1 tablespoon of filling at the base of the leaf and roll up, tucking in the excess leaf at the sides to make a bundle. Remove the core from the cabbage and separate the leaves. Place 1 heaping tablespoon of filling at the base and roll up, tucking in the sides to make a bundle.

Using a heavy-bottomed pot with a lid, line the bottom of the pan with excess cabbage leaves. Place your dolmas on top of the excess cabbage leaves, placing grape leaf dolmas on the bottom and cabbage dolmas on top, with the bottom of your bundles facing down. Dissolve the tomato paste in 1 cup/240 ml of water. Pour the dissolved tomato paste into the pot. Add 3 more cups/700 ml of water. Place an oven-safe, heavy plate over the dolmas to weigh them down. (This is to keep them from unraveling.)

Cover the pot and bring to a light boil. Tilt the lid so the pot is only partially covered. Simmer for 2½ hours. Remove the lid and the plates. Simmer for an additional 30 minutes uncovered.

"SPAGHETTI" WITH MEAT SAUCE

SERVES 6 TO 8

The vegetables and meat make this meal so hearty you won't miss the spaghetti. Plus, this Paleo modification of spaghetti squash will leave you feeling satiated, light and energetic.

INGREDIENTS

FOR THE "SPAGHETTI":

1 large spaghetti squash, halved lengthwise

FOR THE MEAT SAUCE:

2 tbsp/30 g ghee

4 oz/115 g pancetta, finely diced

1 medium yellow onion, finely diced

2 ribs celery, finely diced

1 carrot, peeled and finely diced

¼ tsp pepper

½ tsp sea salt

4 cloves garlic, minced

½ cup/40 g dried porcini mushrooms, rehydrated and chopped

2 lbs/900 g grass-fed ground beef

6 ripe tomatoes, peeled, seeded and chopped (page 212)

3 tbsp/45 ml tomato paste (preferably from a jar)

2 tsp/1 g dried oregano

2 tsp/1 g dried basil

1 cup/235 ml Beef Broth (page 204)

1 bay leaf

fresh basil, chopped (garnish)

COOKING INSTRUCTIONS

Preheat oven to 375°F/190°C. Place squash in a baking dish, cut sides down. Add enough water to come ½-inch/1 cm up the sides of the baking dish. Bake for 45 minutes. Turn the squash over and cook for another 15 minutes. Remove from oven. Allow to cool. Use a spoon to discard seeds from the center. Use a fork to rake the squash to remove its flesh in strands that look like spaghetti.

To make the meat sauce, heat a large skillet to medium-high heat and add ghee. Add pancetta. After it has released some fat, add onion, celery, carrot, pepper and salt. When the vegetables are tender, add garlic and mushrooms and cook for 5 more minutes. Remove the vegetables and set aside.

Put the pan back on the heat and add the meat. Cook until it browns, about 15 minutes. Add the cooked vegetables, tomatoes, tomato paste, oregano and basil. Stir to combine. Add beef broth and bay leaf. Turn heat down to reduce the sauce until the liquid evaporates, about 1 hour. Remove bay leaf. Adjust salt and pepper to taste. Pour over spaghetti squash and garnish with fresh basil.

CHEF'S TIP

This recipe makes quite a bit of sauce. If you don't use it all, you can freeze it for another night!

BALSAMIC ROSEMARY ROASTED CHICKEN AND YAMS

SERVES 4

The balsamic vinegar balances out this one-pot meal by adding the perfect hint of sweetness and acidity. I recommend using a high-quality balsamic vinegar for the best results.

INGREDIENTS

1 whole chicken, cut into 8 pieces

sea salt and pepper

2 tbsp/30 g ghee

1 red onion, sliced

3 cloves garlic, minced

2 tbsp/30 ml balsamic vinegar, preferably an aged, syrupy variety

3 yams, peeled and chopped

2 sprigs rosemary

COOKING INSTRUCTIONS

Preheat oven to 400°F/204°C. Heat a large Dutch oven or a heavy-bottomed, oven-safe pan over medium heat. Generously salt and pepper the chicken. Add 2 tbsp/30 g of ghee to the pan.

Add the chicken to the pan, skin side down. When the skin releases easily, after about 5 minutes, flip and brown the other side for about 3 minutes. Transfer chicken to a plate. Add the onions and sauté until soft, about 5 minutes. Add garlic and sauté until fragrant, about 1 minute. Add the balsamic vinegar and scrape the bottom of the pan with a wooden spoon to get up any brown bits. Turn the heat off the pan. Add the yams and toss with the onion mixture. Generously salt and pepper the mixture. Lay the sprigs of rosemary on top of the yams. Place your browned chicken on top of the rosemary. Cover the pan with a lid and bake for 45 minutes. Turn your oven from bake to broil. Remove the lid and broil for 10 minutes or until your chicken skin is nice and crispy but not burned. Discard rosemary sprigs.

FRUIT-STUFFED CHICKEN

SERVES 4

This is an impressive dish to make for a holiday gathering in the fall, when apples are in season. The sweet and tart flavor of the apples combined with the zesty orange will fill your house with the comforting scents of autumn.

INGREDIENTS

1 roasting chicken (approximately 3½ lbs/1½ kg)

1 large orange

sea salt and pepper

4 tbsp/60 g butter, divided

1 cup/150 g red onion, diced

3 cloves garlic, minced

2 apples, unpeeled, cored and diced

1 tbsp/1 g fresh rosemary, minced, plus a few sprigs

COOKING INSTRUCTIONS

Preheat the oven to 350°F/177°C. Remove any organs from the chicken's cavity and reserve for another use. Rinse the bird with cold water and pat dry. Grate the zest from the orange and reserve. Cut the orange into half and rub all over the chicken. Liberally salt and pepper the entire bird.

Melt butter in a skillet. Add red onion and cook over low heat until tender. Add garlic and apples and sauté until apples are soft but not cooked through, about 10 minutes. Salt and pepper generously. Turn off the heat and combine orange zest and rosemary with the apple and onion mixture.

Stuff the chicken with the mixture. Stuff rosemary sprigs under the skin. Tie the legs together with kitchen twine. Place the chicken breast up in a roasting pan. Dot each breast with a tablespoon of butter. Roast for 1½ hours. Let chicken rest, and carve.

LEMON-GARLIC CHICKEN

SERVES 4

Lemon-Garlic Chicken is our go-to chicken dish; a good friend we can always count on. The flavors are fresh and bright and the dish is versatile enough to serve with almost any vegetables that you have on hand. We sometimes even whip it up quickly after a long day of work, although the flavors are greatly improved when the chicken is properly marinated.

We love to eat this with zucchini noodles and Pistachio Pesto (page 207).

INGREDIENTS

¼ cup/60 ml fresh lemon juice

4 cloves garlic, crushed

1 tbsp/1 g dried parsley

1 tsp/5 g dried basil

½ tsp dried oregano

½ tsp sea salt

¼ tsp pepper

2 lbs/900 g whole chicken legs, bone in, skin removed

2 tbsp/30 ml butter

COOKING INSTRUCTIONS

Combine lemon juice, garlic, parsley, basil, oregano, salt and pepper. Pour over chicken and marinate for at least 1 hour, up to overnight.

Preheat oven to 375°F/190°C. Place chicken pieces in an ovenproof dish, taking care not to overcrowd. Dot several pieces of butter on each piece. Bake for 30 minutes or until a meat thermometer reads 165°F/74°C.

SLOW-COOKER CHOCOLATE CHICKEN MOLE

SERVES 6

I have been perfecting the recipe for a slow-cooker chicken mole for several years. I think I finally got it right! The dark chocolate adds richness and complexity, while the peppers add a smoky flavor and the tomatoes brighten up the dish.

INGREDIENTS

2 lbs/900 g chicken pieces (breasts and legs work well), bone in, skins removed

salt and pepper

2 tbsp/30 g ghee

1 medium onion, chopped

4 cloves garlic, crushed or minced

6–7 whole tomatoes, peeled, seeded and chopped (page 212)

5 dried New Mexico chili peppers, rehydrated and chopped

¼ cup/60 g almond butter

2 ½ oz/70 g dark chocolate (70% or above)

1 tsp/5 g sea salt

1 tsp/3 g cumin

½ tsp ground cinnamon

½ tsp guajillo chili powder

avocado, cilantro and jalapeño, all chopped (garnish)

COOKING INSTRUCTIONS

Generously salt and pepper the chicken. Place a pan over medium heat and add ghee. Once the ghee has warmed, add the chicken and brown on all sides. This may need to be done in batches. Move chicken to the slow cooker.

Add onion to the same pan and sauté until translucent. Add garlic and sauté for 1 to 2 minutes, until fragrant. Transfer onion and garlic to slow cooker. Add the tomatoes, chili peppers, almond butter, dark chocolate, salt and spices (cumin, cinnamon, chili powder) to the slow cooker. Cook on low for 4 to 6 hours or until chicken is tender and pulls apart easily. If you are home when making this dish, lift the lid once and give a stir to make sure all the ingredients are well combined. Remove chicken bones. Top mole with avocado, cilantro and jalapeño and serve!

GRILLED CHICKEN CHERMOULA

SERVES 4

Chermoula is a marinade often used for fish or seafood in Algerian, Moroccan and Tunisian cuisines. The bright flavors of the fresh herbs lend themselves to chicken dishes, too. This dish is best if you allow the chicken to marinate overnight.

INGREDIENTS

6 tbsp/90 ml extra-virgin olive oil

2 tsp/5 g cumin

½ tsp sea salt

½ tsp coriander

½ tsp sweet paprika

1 medium red chili pepper, seeded and chopped

finely grated zest and juice of 1 lemon

2 cloves garlic, crushed

1 ½ cups/40 g fresh cilantro leaves

½ cup/13 g fresh parsley leaves

1 whole chicken, cut into 8 pieces

COOKING INSTRUCTIONS

Combine all ingredients except chicken in a food processor. Blend for 1 minute or until well mixed. Reserve ¼ cup/60 ml of the marinade to serve with the chicken. Pour the rest of the marinade over the cut chicken pieces, making sure they are well coated. Tuck as much marinade as you can under the chicken skin. Cover and set in the fridge for at least 4 hours, up to overnight.

Heat the grill to medium-high. Grill chicken, turning once halfway through. Grill for 30–40 minutes or until internal temperature reads 165°F/74°C. Serve drizzled with extra sauce.

TANDOORI CHICKEN

SERVES 4

Tandoori chicken is an Indian dish, traditionally prepared in a clay oven called a tandoor. You can now find recipes for grilled and roasted variations. This dish is typically prepared with yogurt and spices. I have made this recipe with yogurt and all my taste testers preferred the coconut milk version!

The mild heat from the cayenne in this dish is balanced out by the coconut milk and zesty lemon juice.

INGREDIENTS

1 tsp/5 g fenugreek, whole

1 tsp/5 g peppercorn, whole

1 tsp/5 g coriander

1 tsp/3 g cumin

1 tsp/3 g garam masala

½ tsp cayenne

¼ tsp turmeric

1 tsp/5 g sea salt

1 inch/2 cm fresh ginger, minced

1 jalapeño, minced

2 tbsp/30 ml fresh lemon juice

½ cup/118 ml coconut milk

2 lbs/907 g chicken legs and thigh, bone in, skin removed

COOKING INSTRUCTIONS

Preheat your oven to 375°F/190°C. Place fenugreek and peppercorn through a spice grinder. In a small bowl mix the fenugreek, peppercorn, coriander, cumin, garam masala, cayenne, turmeric and salt. Next, mix in the ginger, jalapeño, lemon juice and coconut milk. Stir until well mixed.

Make a few deep slashes in each piece of chicken. This will help the chicken absorb more of the flavor. Pour the spice mixture over the chicken. Make sure the chicken is well coated. Place in fridge for at least 4 hours, up to overnight.

Preheat oven to 375°F/190°C. Place chicken on a wire rack on top of a baking sheet so the baking sheet catches the drippings. Cook for 50-60 minutes or until a meat thermometer reads 165°F/74°C.

MACADAMIA-CRUSTED DUCK BREAST WITH SPICY "SOY" GINGER SAUCE

SERVES 4

Coconut aminos are a great Paleo substitute for soy sauce. They have a similar salty flavor, with a slight hint of sweetness. I use real soy sauce made from fermented soybeans as a condiment. Soybeans have a high level of phytates, which tend to block the body's absorption of minerals. However, fermentation substantially reduces levels of phytic acid, so fermented soy is preferable.

In recipes such as this one, I prefer the subtler flavor of coconut aminos to soy sauce. The bold flavors of this spicy sauce complement the creaminess and rich flavor of the duck.

INGREDIENTS

1 cup/120 g macadamia nuts

4 duck breast halves, boneless, skin on

sea salt and pepper

1 tbsp/15 g duck fat or ghee

2 tsp/15 g raw honey

FOR THE SAUCE:

1 cup/240 g shallots, diced

2 cloves garlic, minced

1 jalapeño, minced

1 tbsp/8 g fresh ginger, grated

¼ cup/60 ml coconut aminos

2 tbsp/30 ml fresh lime juice

1 tsp/7 g raw honey

COOKING INSTRUCTIONS

Preheat oven to 350°F/177°C. Place macadamia nuts in a food processor and blend until crushed. Heat a skillet, preferably cast iron, over medium-high heat. Generously season both sides of the duck breasts with salt and pepper. Add the duck fat or ghee to the pan, then add the duck skin-side down. Brown until the skin has a nice golden crust, about 5 minutes. Flip over and brown the other side for 1 to 2 minutes.

Transfer the duck breasts to a glass baking dish, skin-side up. Allow to cool for a few minutes. Spoon ½ teaspoon of honey on the skin side of each duck breast. Spoon enough of the crushed macadamia nuts over the honey so the entire top of the duck breast is covered. Make sure the breast is well coated. Do this to the remaining duck breasts. Place in the oven and roast for 20 minutes medium well.

While the duck breasts are roasting, make the sauce. Using the same pan that the duck was seared in, drain all but about 1 tablespoon/15 ml of fat. Add the shallots. Cook until soft, about 5 minutes. Add the garlic, jalapeño and ginger. Sauté until fragrant, about 1 minute. Stir in the coconut aminos, lime juice and honey. Simmer until slightly reduced. Adjust salt to taste. Remove duck breast from the oven, let rest for 5 minutes and serve drizzled with sauce.

WINE-BRAISED DUCK LEGS

SERVES 4

I recommend buying whole ducks for this dish. Buying a whole duck is more cost-effective and almost all of the parts can be used. Use the breasts to make my Macadamia-Crusted Duck Breast with Spicy "Soy" Ginger Sauce (page 88), the skin to render for duck fat, and the carcass to make stock.

INGREDIENTS

½ bunch fresh parsley

½ bunch fresh thyme

1 tsp/5 g sea salt

½ tsp pepper

¼ tsp red chili flakes

4 duck legs

2 tbsp/30 g duck fat or ghee

1 large onion, diced

1 carrot, peeled and diced

2 cloves garlic, minced

1 cup/235 ml dry red wine

1 cup/160 g tomatoes, peeled, seeded and diced

1 bay leaf

2 cups/475 ml Chicken Broth (page 202)

2 tbsp/30 g butter

kitchen twine

COOKING INSTRUCTIONS

Preheat oven to 375°F/190°C. Tie the parsley and thyme together with some kitchen twine. Combine the salt, pepper and red chili flakes in a small bowl. Rub each duck leg on the meat side with the mixture. Heat the duck fat or ghee in a Dutch oven or a large, ovenproof, heavy-bottomed pan. Add the duck legs, skin-side down, and sear until lightly browned, about 3 minutes. Turn the duck legs over and sear the other side, about 2 minutes. Transfer to a platter and set aside.

If there is too much fat in the pan, drain all but 2 tablespoons/30 ml. Add the onion and carrots and sauté for 5 minutes. Add the garlic and sauté for an additional minute. Add the wine and tomatoes and bring to a light boil, scraping up any brown bits from the bottom of the pan. Add the thyme, parsley, bay leaf and chicken broth.

Place the duck legs skin side down in the pan. Cover and place in the oven to cook for 1½ hours. Halfway through, flip the duck legs so the skin side is up. Change your oven setting to broil and cook uncovered for the last 10 minutes. Remove duck legs and strain the sauce through a sieve and into a sauté pan. Bring the liquid to a boil, then turn down to a simmer and reduce it by half or to desired consistency. Turn off the heat, stir in the butter and adjust salt to taste. Put the duck on individual plates, spoon the sauce over and serve.

JAMAICAN JERK PORK CHOPS

SERVES 4

When I started the Paleo diet, one of my closest friends brought me some jerk seasoning from Jamaica. I read the ingredients and noticed a few questionable items, so I decided to make my own. This is what I came up with!

INGREDIENTS

2 scallions, chopped

2 cloves garlic, minced

1 tbsp/8 g fresh ginger, peeled and grated

1 serrano chili pepper, seeded and minced

1 tbsp/20 g raw honey

1 tbsp/6 g allspice

1 tbsp/2 g dried thyme

1 tsp/8 g ground cinnamon

1 tsp/3 g ground nutmeg

¼ tsp cayenne pepper

1 tsp/5 g sea salt

1 tsp/5 g pepper

juice of 1 lime

juice of 1 orange

2 tbsp/30 ml coconut vinegar

2 tbsp/15 g coconut aminos

¼ cup/60 ml extra-virgin olive oil

2 tbsp/30 ml coconut oil

4 pork chops, bone in

COOKING INSTRUCTIONS

Combine all of the ingredients in a bowl except the coconut oil and pork. Make sure it is all mixed well. Place pork chops in a shallow bowl and pour marinade over the chops. Cover and marinate for at least 1 hour, up to overnight.

Heat the coconut oil in a large skillet over medium heat. When it has melted, remove the pork chops from the marinade and place in the skillet, making sure they are not crowding each other. If your skillet is not large enough, you may need to do this in batches. Cook 3–4 minutes per side; the length will depend on the thickness of your chops. Flip over as soon as one side is well browned.

PORK CHOPS WITH POMEGRANATE-GINGER SAUCE

SERVES 4

Pomegranates are one of the most recognizable symbols of Armenia; they represent fertility, abundance and marriage. Pomegranate season was a special time for us growing up. My younger brother and I always looked forward to sitting at the dining table and enjoying the seeds that our mom had carefully removed.

Now I enjoy leveraging their unique and tantalizing flavor to elevate simple meals like these panfried pork chops.

INGREDIENTS

FOR THE SAUCE:

½ cup/120 ml unsweetened pomegranate juice

½ cup/120 ml Chicken Broth (page 202)

½ cup/120 g shallots, diced

1 clove garlic, minced

1 tsp/5 g fresh ginger, minced

1 tbsp/20 g raw honey

3 sprigs thyme

Dash of sea salt

1 tsp/2 g arrowroot starch

1 tsp/3 g coriander

½ tsp onion powder

½ tsp garlic powder

4 pork chops, center cut

sea salt and pepper

2 tbsp/30 ml coconut oil

COOKING INSTRUCTIONS

In a medium-sized saucepan, combine all of the ingredients for the pomegranate-ginger sauce, except the arrowroot starch. Cook until reduced by half, about 10 minutes. Remove sauce from the heat and set aside. Once the sauce is cool, strain it through a fine mesh strainer to remove the solids.

In a small bowl, mix coriander, onion powder and garlic powder. Rub the seasonings mix on both sides of the pork chops. Generously salt and pepper.

Heat a large skillet to medium-high heat. Once the pan is hot add the coconut oil. Place the chops in the pan and make sure that they are not crowding each other too much. Cook chops on each side for about 4 minutes or until well browned and cooked through. Remove the chops from the pan and set aside to rest.

As your chops are resting, add the strained pomegranate-ginger sauce to the same pan and bring to a simmer. Stir for a couple of minutes and scrape up any browned bits. Place your arrowroot starch in a small bowl and add enough filtered water to make a thin paste. Add this paste to the sauce and whisk until the sauce is slightly thickened. Spoon the warm sauce over the pork chops and serve.

CITRUS-BRAISED PORK SHOULDER

SERVES 6 TO 8

Not many meals can compare to a blissfully tender and moist pork shoulder. This informal dish is so versatile and can easily be dressed up with some sophisticated sides.

When purchasing lard, read labels carefully to ensure that the only ingredient is rendered pork fat. Lard from pasture-raised pigs is a great source of vitamin D!

INGREDIENTS

FOR THE RUB:

1 tbsp/8 g cumin

2 tsp/5 g coriander

½ tsp dried oregano

½ tsp paprika

1 tsp/5 g sea salt

½ tsp pepper

3 lbs/1 kg boneless pork shoulder

2 tbsp/30 g lard or ghee

1 onion, chopped

4 cloves garlic, minced

¼ cup/60 ml of fresh lime juice

½ cup/120 ml of fresh orange juice

2 bay leaves

3 cups/710 ml of Chicken Broth (page 202)

COOKING INSTRUCTIONS

Preheat oven to 350°F/177°C. In a small bowl, mix all ingredients for the rub until well combined. Sprinkle the rub over the pork shoulder, then rub the pork with the seasoning until all sides are well coated. Heat a Dutch oven or a heavy, oven-safe pot over medium heat. Add the lard or ghee. Once it is hot, add the pork shoulder. Brown the pork shoulder on all sides, approximately 2 to 3 minutes per side. Set aside.

Add the onions to the same pan and sauté until soft, about 5 minutes. Add the garlic and sauté until fragrant. Add the lime juice and orange juice, and use a wooden spoon to scrape up any brown bits from the bottom of the pan. Next add bay leaves and chicken broth. Cover and place the roast in the oven for 2½ hours. Baste the pork twice while it is cooking. Remove the cover for the last 15 minutes to allow the pork to brown. Discard bay leaves before serving.

CHINESE FIVE-SPICE PLUM PORK RIBS

SERVES 4

While no one knows its exact origins, some believe that the Chinese created five-spice powder to encompass all of the five flavors: sour, bitter, sweet, pungent and salty. These five elements combined create a powerful flavor. The five-spice brings a unique flavor to this dish. Remember when using it, a little goes a long way!

INGREDIENTS

2 tbsp/40 g raw honey

⅓ cup/80 ml fresh orange juice

1 tsp/2 g Chinese five-spice powder

1 tsp/5 g fresh ginger, minced

1 serrano pepper, minced

3 cloves garlic, minced

1 tsp/5 g sea salt

2 lbs/900 g pork spare ribs, cut into 4 slabs

1 lb/455 g plums, pitted and halved or, if very large, quartered

COOKING INSTRUCTIONS

Preheat the oven to 300°F/150°C. In a small bowl, mix all the ingredients except ribs and plums until well combined. Place ribs meat-side down in an oven-safe pan with a lid, such as a Dutch oven. Pour sauce over the ribs and make sure they are well coated. Arrange the cut plums around the ribs. Cover and bake for 2 hours. Halfway through remove the lid and baste the pork.

Increase the oven to 375°F/190°C. Remove the cover and flip the pork so the meat is facing up. Bake for an additional 15 to 20 minutes or until ribs are browned. Place ribs on a plate with some plums and drizzle with sauce.

BRAISED GOAT SHOULDER

SERVES 8

Goat is the most widely consumed red meat in the world, a staple among many cultures but rarely eaten in the United States. I am not sure why, because it is truly delicious! Pasture-raised goat meat tastes more like beef than lamb. Because goat is very lean, the shoulder can be quite tough, but becomes tender and tasty when braised with moist heat. Next time you see some goat at your farmers' market, pick some up and give this recipe a try!

INGREDIENTS

2 tbsp/30 g ghee

sea salt and pepper

3 lbs/1 kg boneless goat shoulder

1 onion, thinly sliced

2 tbsp/30 ml tomato paste (preferably from a jar)

4 cloves garlic, minced

1 leek, thinly sliced

1 rib celery, diced

1 carrot, peeled and diced

1 tbsp/15 ml red wine vinegar

4 cups/945 ml Beef Broth (page 204)

6 ripe tomatoes, quartered

4 sprigs thyme

2 bay leaves

COOKING INSTRUCTIONS

Preheat oven to 375°F/190°C. Heat a large Dutch oven to medium-high heat and add ghee. Generously salt and pepper the goat shoulder. When the ghee is warm, add the meat and brown on all sides, about 5 minutes on the first side. Set the meat aside.

Add the onion to the Dutch oven and cook until soft, about 5 minutes. Add the tomato paste, garlic, leek, celery and carrot. Cook for a few minutes until fragrant. Add the red wine vinegar and scrape up any brown bits from the pan. Add the broth, tomatoes, thyme and bay leaves. Cover and place in the oven. Cook for 2 hours or until goat shoulder is tender. Discard thyme sprigs and bay leaves before serving.

SLOW-COOKER LAMB VINDALOO

SERVES 6

My grandma taught me that food always tastes best when it is made from scratch. Although I have curry pastes in my pantry for when I am short on time, I always jump at an opportunity to make my own. This exquisite spicy curry dish is surprisingly simple to make.

INGREDIENTS

FOR THE PASTE:

6 dried chili peppers

½ yellow onion, diced

4 cloves garlic, crushed

2 tsp/10 g fresh ginger, grated

1 tsp/3 g ground cinnamon

½ tsp ground cloves

¼ tsp ground turmeric

1 tbsp/8 g coriander

1 tbsp/8 g cumin

1 tsp/5 g fenugreek

1 tsp/5 g sea salt

2 tbsp/30 ml distilled white vinegar

2 lbs/900 g of lamb (shoulder or stew meat)

2 tbsp/30 g of ghee

½ cup/120 ml Beef Broth (page 204)

COOKING INSTRUCTIONS

Soak chili peppers in warm water for 30 minutes. In a food processor, combine chili peppers and all other paste ingredients. Spread the paste over the lamb and marinate for at least several hours, up to overnight. Brown the lamb in 2 tablespoons/28 g of ghee. This may have to be done in batches. Place lamb with remaining paste in the slow cooker and add broth. Cook on low for 6–8 hours.

LAMB SHANKS WITH APRICOTS

SERVES 6

It is difficult to describe the distinct flavor of saffron. For me, it has a nostalgic flavor, reminding me of the many dishes that I enjoyed growing up. If you have never cooked with saffron, one thing to note is that a little goes a long way. This is a good thing, as it is the most expensive spice in the world!

Juicy and sweet apricots are the perfect accompaniment to the pungent saffron in this dish.

INGREDIENTS

FOR THE RUB:

½ tsp ground ginger

½ tsp allspice

1 tsp/3 g cumin

¼ tsp turmeric

¼ tsp cayenne

½ tsp lemon zest

3 lbs/1 kg lamb shanks

sea salt and pepper

3 tbsp/45 ml ghee

1 red onion, sliced

5 garlic cloves, minced

3-4 cups/710-945 ml Beef Broth (page 204)

2 strands saffron

2 cups/360 g fresh apricots, pitted and halved (or ½ cup/75 g dried, chopped)

COOKING INSTRUCTIONS

Preheat oven to 400°F/204°C. Combine all the ingredients for the rub and rub all over the lamb. Generously season with salt and pepper. Heat a Dutch oven to medium-high heat. Add the ghee. Once it is hot, brown lamb on all sides. Remove the lamb and set aside.

Sauté the onion in the same Dutch oven until soft, about 5 minutes, and then add the garlic. Cook for a minute or two. Add the broth, bring to a boil and scrape the bottom of the pan to get up any brown bits. Add the saffron and apricots. Return the meat and cover and place into preheated oven. Cook for 1½ to 2 hours or until shanks have become tender. Turn the shanks over halfway through cooking. Remove the lid for the last 20 minutes to allow the shanks to get a nice brown crust. Serve the lamb shanks with the cooked apricots and drizzled with juice from the pan.

SUN-DRIED TOMATO AND MUSHROOM LAMB BURGERS

SERVES 6

When it comes to burgers, most people think of beef. Lamb offers cooks a more complex and sophisticated flavor to work with. The sweet and savory sun-dried tomatoes and earthy mushrooms harmonize perfectly with the rich lamb. My favorite way to enjoy burgers is on top of grilled portobello mushrooms.

INGREDIENTS

½ cup/80 g sun-dried tomatoes, chopped

½ cup/40 g dried porcini mushrooms, chopped

2 lbs/900 g ground lamb

2 pieces bacon, chopped

4 cloves garlic, minced

½ onion, grated

1 tsp/3 g chili powder

2 tsp/10 g sea salt

½ tsp pepper

½ cup/20 g fresh parsley

¼ cup/5 g fresh basil

1 jalapeño, minced

1 egg, lightly beaten

FOR THE PORTOBELLO MUSHROOMS:

6 portobello mushrooms, stemmed

sea salt and pepper

2 tbsp/30 g butter, melted

COOKING INSTRUCTIONS

Rehydrate sun-dried tomatoes by placing them in a bowl and covering them with warm water. Let them soak at room temperature for at least 45 minutes or until they feel flexible. Rehydrate dried mushrooms by placing them in a bowl and covering them with warm water for 30 to 45 minutes.

Preheat a grill over medium-high heat. Combine the sun-dried tomatoes, mushrooms, lamb, bacon, garlic, onion, chili powder, salt, pepper, parsley, basil, jalapeño and egg. Mix gently. Form into 6 patties. Remove the stems from the portobello mushrooms. Generously salt and pepper them and liberally brush with melted butter. Grill burgers for about 4 minutes a side for medium burgers. Cook portobello mushrooms for 5 minutes per side or until heated through and tender. Top each portobello mushroom with a burger and serve.

CHEF'S TIP
For an added flavor boost, top this burger with sautéed onions and sliced avocado.

GRILLED LAMB CHOPS WITH MINT PESTO

SERVES 6

Armenian and Persian cooking liberally use fresh herbs, fruits and nuts. Even when I am not making a Middle Eastern dish, the influence on my cooking is very noticeable. I am drawn to developing recipes centered around herbs, such as pestos, chimichurri and herb sauces.

INGREDIENTS

2 lbs/907 g lamb

1 tbsp/15 ml extra-virgin olive oil

2 tbsp/30 ml fresh orange juice

2 tbsp/3 g mint leaves, minced

½ tsp fresh thyme

½ tsp pepper

½ tsp sea salt

3 cloves garlic, minced

½ tsp finely grated orange zest

2 lbs/900 g lamb loin chops, about 8 to 10 chops, cut individually

FOR THE MINT PESTO:

½ cup/15 g mint leaves

¼ cup/5 g fresh basil

¼ cup/30 g macadamia nuts

1 tbsp/10 g garlic, minced

¼ cup/60 ml extra-virgin olive oil

2 tbsp/30 ml fresh lemon juice

1 tbsp/15 ml fresh orange juice

¼ tsp sea salt

¼ tsp pepper

COOKING INSTRUCTIONS

Preheat grill to medium-high. In a small bowl, combine olive oil, orange juice, mint, thyme, pepper, salt, garlic and orange zest. Rub the mixture all over the lamb and let it rest at room temperature for 30 minutes.

In the meantime, prepare the mint pesto by placing all of the ingredients in a food processor and pulsing a few times until well combined. Adjust salt and pepper to taste.

Grill the lamb chops 3 to 4 minutes per side for medium. Serve the lamb chops drizzled with mint pesto.

MEDITERRANEAN STUFFED PEPPERS

SERVES 4

Vibrant peppers are packed with bright and fragrant flavors. A light salad is the perfect accompaniment to this flavorful dish.

INGREDIENTS

1 tbsp/15 g ghee

½ yellow onion, chopped

¼ cup/40 g sun-dried tomatoes, chopped

2 cloves garlic, crushed

1 tbsp/15 ml tomato paste (preferably from a jar)

1 lb/455 g ground lamb

½ tsp sea salt

¼ tsp pepper

¼ cup/10 g fresh parsley, chopped

1 tbsp/2 g mint, chopped

3 red bell peppers, halved and cores removed

COOKING INSTRUCTIONS

Rehydrate sun-dried tomatoes by placing them in a bowl and covering them with warm water. Let them soak at room temperature for at least 45 minutes or until they feel flexible.

Preheat oven to 350°F/177°C. Heat a heavy-bottomed skillet to medium-high heat and add ghee. Add onions and sauté until soft, about 5 minutes. Add sun-dried tomatoes, garlic and tomato paste. Sauté for 1 minute. Add lamb, salt and pepper and cook until browned, using a wooden spoon to break up the clumps. Turn off the heat and fold in the parsley and mint. Use a slotted spoon to pick up the mixture from the pan, leaving the extra fat behind.

Stuff the peppers, place in an oven-safe baking dish and cook for 20 minutes or until meat is browned and peppers are soft.

GINGER LIME BUTTER-SAUTÉED SHRIMP

SERVES 4

Aromatic and spicy ginger paired with tart lime give the shrimp a unique and zesty flavor.

INGREDIENTS

salt and pepper

1 lb/455 g uncooked shrimp, peeled and deveined

2 tbsp/30 g butter

¼ cup/60 g shallots, minced

2 garlic cloves, minced

1 tbsp/15 g fresh ginger, minced

½ tsp/2 ml crushed red pepper flakes

3 tbsp/45 ml fresh lime juice

1 tsp/5 ml lime zest

¼ cup/60 ml coconut amino

2 tbsp/5 g scallions, chopped (garnish)

COOKING INSTRUCTIONS

Generously salt and pepper the shrimp and set aside. In a large skillet, heat the butter over medium heat. When the butter is melted, add the shallots and sauté until soft, about 5 minutes. Add the garlic and ginger and cook until fragrant, about 1 minute. Add the crushed red pepper and cook for 30 seconds. Add the lime juice, lime zest and coconut amino and stir to combine.

Add the shrimp and cook, stirring occasionally, until white throughout, about 4 minutes. Make sure the shrimp is well coated with the sauce. Spoon the shrimp and sauce into shallow bowls and serve topped with scallions.

PANFRIED HALIBUT WITH AVOCADO SALSA

SERVES 4

Incredibly quick to make, this is one of my favorite meals to enjoy after a day at the beach. The avocado salsa is so refreshing.

INGREDIENTS

FOR THE AVOCADO SALSA:

2 scallions, chopped

1 small jalapeño, minced

¼ cup/40 g cherry tomatoes, halved

¼ cup/10 g cilantro, chopped

3 cloves garlic, minced

¼ tsp sea salt

¼ tsp pepper

⅛ tsp cumin

3 tbsp/45 ml fresh lemon juice

2 avocados, peeled and chopped

2 tbsp/30 g butter

sea salt and pepper

4 halibut filets, 4 oz/115 g each

COOKING INSTRUCTIONS

In a medium bowl, combine scallions, jalapeño, cherry tomatoes, cilantro, garlic, salt, pepper, cumin and lemon juice. Fold in avocados, taking care not to smash. Heat a large frying pan over medium-low heat. Add butter. Generously salt and pepper the halibut. Once the butter is warm, cook the halibut until lightly browned, about 5 minutes. Flip and cook until the fish is cooked through, opaque and flakes easily, about 3 minutes. Top with avocado salsa and serve.

PAN-ROASTED HALIBUT WITH MUSHROOMS AND LEEKS

SERVES 4

The smooth, buttery texture of halibut is complemented by the delicate flavor of the leek and the earthy flavor of the mushrooms. This dish is relatively quick to make, ideal for a weeknight dinner and fancy enough to serve to guests.

INGREDIENTS

2 tbsp/30 g unsalted butter

4 cups/300 g crimini mushrooms, sliced

2 large leeks, white and light green parts only, thinly sliced

sea salt and pepper

4 skinless halibut fillets (about 4 oz/115 g each)

5 sprigs fresh thyme

1 tbsp/2 g fresh flat-leaf parsley (garnish)

COOKING INSTRUCTIONS

Heat a large skillet with a lid over medium heat. Melt the butter and add the mushrooms and leeks. Season with salt and pepper. Cook carefully until leeks and mushrooms are softened but not browned. Generously season the halibut with salt and pepper and nestle the fish among the vegetables in the skillet. Add the thyme. Cover tightly. Cook gently until the fish is just cooked through, about 7 minutes. Discard thyme sprigs. Serve the fish with mushrooms and leeks, topped with fresh parsley.

CHEF'S TIP
Freeze the green parts of the leeks to add to stocks and broths (pages 202-204).

SLOW-COOKED MACADAMIA ROSEMARY SALMON

SERVES 6 TO 8

I can't recall where I picked up this method of cooking salmon, but it's become my favorite technique. This method does take a bit longer, but the end result is a tender, juicy and silky fish.

INGREDIENTS

1 3–lb/1-kg salmon fillet

2 tbsp/30 ml macadamia nut oil

½ tsp sea salt

¼ tsp pepper

3 sprigs fresh rosemary

4 cloves garlic, minced

1 whole lemon, sliced

COOKING INSTRUCTIONS

Preheat oven to 200°F/93°C. Place a pan of warm water on the lowest rack to keep the heat moist. Place the salmon in a baking dish. Lightly brush the salmon with macadamia nut oil. Season with salt and pepper, top with rosemary sprigs, garlic and, lastly, slices of lemon. Cook for 1 hour. Do not open the oven often, since it is set at such a low heat. Serve.

STEAMED SALMON WITH CURRIED PEAR AND MANGO CHUTNEY

SERVES 4

The curry powder and the lemon juice combine to give this chutney a bold flavor, a perfect complement to a simply steamed salmon fillet.

INGREDIENTS

1 tbsp/15 g ghee

¼ cup/40 g red onion, diced

1 small pear, peeled, cored and finely diced

1 ripe mango, peeled and finely diced

1 serrano pepper, minced

1 large or 2 small garlic cloves, minced

2 tbsp/10 g dried cherries, rehydrated and finely diced

2 tsp/15 g raw honey

2 tsp/10 g fresh ginger, grated

1 tsp/3 g spicy curry powder, divided

¼ cup/60 ml fresh lemon juice

¼ cup/60 ml fresh lime juice

4 6-oz/170-g salmon fillets

sea salt and pepper

COOKING INSTRUCTIONS

Warm a heavy-bottomed frying pan over medium heat. Add the ghee. Add the onion and cook until translucent, 3 to 4 minutes. Toss in the pear, mango, pepper, garlic, dried cherries, honey, ginger and ½ teaspoon curry powder. Cook for 1 to 2 minutes. Add the lemon and lime juices and bring to a simmer. Cook until the chutney is reduced by half. Remove from the heat and set aside. This can be made in advance and reheated before serving, or it can be served at room temperature.

Generously season the salmon with salt and pepper, and with the remaining curry powder. Place a steamer basket in a large pot. Bring a small amount of water to a boil. The water should not come into the basket. Place the salmon fillets on the steamer tray, skin-side down. Cover and steam until the fish is opaque, about 10 minutes. Serve the salmon topped with chutney.

PANFRIED COD WITH HERB SAUCE

SERVES 4

Mild-flavored cod is the perfect pairing for this herb sauce. The fish takes a backseat and allows the sauce to be the star of the show. Cod is often dredged in flour, but I prefer fresh cod to be lightly seasoned with salt and pepper and panfried with some butter.

INGREDIENTS

FOR THE SAUCE:

4 tbsp/10 g fresh parsley, coarsely chopped

1 tbsp/3 g mint leaves

1 tbsp/3 g fresh basil leaves

1 tbsp/3 g scallions, chopped

1 tbsp/8 g tarragon

1 medium red chili, chopped

3 tbsp/45 ml extra-virgin olive oil

1 clove garlic

2 tbsp/30 ml lemon juice

sea salt and pepper

2 tbsp/30 g butter

sea salt and pepper

4 6-oz/170-g cod fillets, without skin

COOKING INSTRUCTIONS

Make the herb sauce. Pulse all of the ingredients in a food processor. Adjust salt and pepper to taste. Set aside.

Heat a large skillet to medium-high and add butter. Generously salt and pepper the cod. Cook until crisp and golden, about 4 minutes per side. Top with herb sauce and serve.

THAI COCONUT CURRIED MUSSELS

SERVES 2

Wild mussels have a mild, delicate flavor and are slightly chewy. They are easily influenced by the flavors in which they are cooked. The Thai coconut curry broth provides a bright and bold flavor.

INGREDIENTS

1 lb/455 g mussels

1 stalk lemongrass

2 tbsp/30 ml coconut oil

⅓ cup/80 g shallots, sliced

1 tbsp/10 g garlic, minced

2 tsp/10 g fresh ginger, peeled and minced

1 tbsp/15 ml red curry paste

2 cups/475 ml coconut milk (for homemade page 207)

½ cup/120 ml chicken stock

½ tsp lime zest

1 tbsp/15 ml fresh lime juice

2 Thai red peppers, chopped

2 tsp/10 ml fish sauce

2 kaffir lime leaves

¼ cup/7 g cilantro, minced (garnish)

COOKING INSTRUCTIONS

Discard any damaged or open mussels. Soak the mussels in fresh water for 20 minutes. Remove the tougher outer leaves of the lemongrass until you get to the soft, yellow stalk. Trim off the bulb and slice up the yellow, fleshy parts of the lemongrass. Place the lemongrass in a food processor and process well on high. Individually remove each mussel from the water, trim the beard and set in another bowl of clean, cold water.

Heat the coconut oil in a sauté pan over medium heat. Add the shallots and sauté until soft, about 5 minutes. Add the lemongrass, garlic, ginger and red curry paste and sauté for 1 to 2 minutes. Add the coconut milk, chicken stock, lime zest, lime juice, Thai peppers, fish sauce and lime leaves. Cook for 8 to 10 minutes. Add the mussels. Cover and cook over medium heat until the mussels open, 3 to 5 minutes. Discard lime leaves. Uncover and spoon the opened mussels into serving bowls along with the broth. Garnish with cilantro.

PANFRIED MACKEREL WITH GREEN OLIVE RELISH

SERVES 4

Mackerel is one of the most underrated fish, and perhaps for this reason is quite inexpensive. Mackerel is a nutrition powerhouse. In addition to being high in omega-3 fats, it is loaded with minerals such as calcium, phosphorous, potassium, selenium and magnesium, and vitamins such as A, D, K, niacin, B12, Vitamin C, choline and folate.

INGREDIENTS

FOR THE RELISH:

¼ cup/60 g shallots, diced

filtered water

½ cup/90 g green olives, pitted

½ tsp lemon zest

1 tbsp/3 g fresh parsley

1 tbsp/3 g chives

½ cup/75 g watercress

2 tbsp/30 ml fresh lemon juice

2 tbsp/30 ml extra-virgin olive oil

¼ tsp sea salt

¼ tsp pepper

2 tbsp/30 g butter

6 4-oz/115-g mackerel fillets

COOKING INSTRUCTIONS

Cover shallots with filtered water and let sit for 10 minutes. Strain liquid. This will help take the bite out, so the shallots don't overwhelm the rest of the relish. Combine all of the ingredients for the relish in a food processor. Pulse a few times to combine, but do not overblend. Set aside.

Heat the butter in a large frying pan and fry the mackerel for 2 to 3 minutes per side. Serve topped with the green olive relish.

THAI GREEN CURRY CHICKEN

SERVES 6

Thai food is my absolute favorite. I dream of one day eating my way through Thailand, and keeping it Paleo of course! We used to love getting takeout from Thai restaurants, but like most foods, now I prefer to make it at home myself. This green curry chicken bursts with flavor.

INGREDIENTS

1 tbsp/15 ml coconut oil

2 green onions, chopped

3 cloves garlic, minced

1 tsp/3 g fresh ginger, grated

1 tbsp/15 ml coconut aminos

1 tbsp/30 g fish sauce

3 tbps/45 ml green curry paste

3 cups/700 ml coconut milk (for homemade, see page 207)

2 lbs/900 g, boneless and skinless chicken thighs

2 kaffir lime leaves

1 small jalapeño, chopped (optional)

¼ tsp sea salt

½ of a fresh lime

cilantro for garnish

COOKING INSTRUCTIONS

Heat coconut oil in a large sauté pan with a tight-fitting lid over medium heat. Sauté the green onion until soft, about 3 minutes. Then add the garlic, ginger, coconut aminos, fish sauce and curry paste and cook for an additional minute, until fragrant. Pour in the coconut milk, kaffir lime leaves, jalapeños and salt. Lay the chicken pieces in the mixture to poach. Bring the mixture to a simmer. Reduce to low heat and cook with the lid on for 50 minutes, or until chicken pulls apart with a fork easily. Pull the chicken apart, use a slotted spoon to remove it from the coconut milk. Squeeze in the lime juice and shower with chopped cilantro.

CHEF'S TIP

Use the remaining broth to cook vegetables for a side dish. Cook vegetables over medium heat until soft. Yams, carrots and zucchini all work well!

Chapter 5

SIMPLY *Sensational* SALADS

Sometimes there is nothing more satisfying than a salad loaded with fresh produce and even fruit. Salads offer so much opportunity for creativity in the kitchen. Well-stocked with local organic produce from our farmers' markets and CSAs, we never tire of opening the fridge and throwing together a new salad combination. Most nights you will find a salad of sorts on our dinner table.

Salads can be served as a starter to a meal, or can be substantial enough to be enjoyed for lunch or dinner on their own. I have been experimenting with salads for a long time. They are the one thing I didn't stop making when I took a cooking hiatus in my early 20s. In college, I was known for the hefty and satisfying salads that I would regularly make for my friends and roommates.

Here I have included a variety of salads that can be served alongside comfort foods, can be the start to an elegant dinner or can be enjoyed at a summer potluck!

BEET-GREEN SALAD

SERVES 4

If you include any dairy in your diet, the addition of burrata, a creamy, fresh Italian cheese, elevates this salad to the next level.

INGREDIENTS

6 beets

sea salt

1 tbsp/15 ml extra-virgin olive oil

Leaves from 2 bunches of beets, roughly chopped

FOR THE VINAIGRETTE:

1 tbsp/15 g shallot, finely chopped

2 tbsp/30 ml champagne vinegar

2 tbsp/30 ml fresh orange juice

2 tbsp/30 ml fresh lemon juice

¼ tsp lemon zest

1 tsp/5 g stone-ground mustard

1 tsp/7 g raw honey

sea salt and pepper to taste

¼ cup/60 ml extra-virgin olive oil

2 tomatoes, sliced into 1-inch/2-cm wedges

1 cup/180 g cucumber, half peeled and chopped

COOKING INSTRUCTIONS

Preheat oven to 400°F/204°C. Wash, dry and trim beets. Reserve beet greens. Place beets in a shallow baking dish. Sprinkle with sea salt and drizzle with olive oil. Bake for 40 minutes. Let the cooked beets cool for 5 minutes. Place a steamer basket in a large pot. Bring a small amount of water to a boil. The water should not come into the basket. Place beet leaves in the basket and steam for 5 to 7 minutes or until soft. Peel the beets by using a paper towel to slide the skin right off. Cut each beet into quarters and set aside.

Make the citrus vinaigrette by mixing all ingredients except olive oil in a medium bowl. Slowly whisk in olive oil. Adjust salt and pepper to taste. Arrange beets, beet greens, tomatoes and cucumbers on 4 separate plates. Sprinkle with sea salt and drizzle with citrus vinaigrette.

ASPARAGUS SALAD WITH LEMON-BASIL VINAIGRETTE

SERVES 8

Blanching is my favorite way to prepare asparagus for salads. Quickly blanching them doesn't give them the opportunity to overcook and get mushy. This light salad accompanied by my Lemon-Garlic Chicken (page 82) is perfect for a summer lunch.

INGREDIENTS

FOR THE VINAIGRETTE:

4 tbsp/60 ml fresh Meyer lemon juice

1 tsp/3 g lemon zest

1 tbsp/15 ml champagne vinegar

1 small clove garlic, minced

1 tsp/7 g raw honey

½ tsp sea salt

¼ tsp pepper

3 tbsp/5 g fresh basil, finely chopped

¼ cup/60 ml extra-virgin olive oil

2 lbs/900 g asparagus

COOKING INSTRUCTIONS

To make the vinaigrette, combine everything except the olive oil. Then slowly whisk in olive oil. Break off tough ends from the asparagus and discard. Cut asparagus into 2-inch/5-cm pieces. Bring a large pot of salted water to a boil. Once water is boiling, add asparagus and cook for 2 minutes. Drain liquid and place in a bowl of cold water to stop cooking. Toss with lemon-basil vinaigrette. Serve immediately or chill in the refrigerator.

CHEF'S TIP

If you don't have Meyer lemon, substitute 3 tbsp/44 ml regular lemon juice, plus 1 tbsp/15 ml orange juice.

SPICY WATERMELON AND MINT SALAD

SERVES 8

This sweet, spicy and tangy salad is a perfect accompaniment to BBQ!

INGREDIENTS

1 cup/150 g red onion, chopped

Filtered water

4 cups/720 g seedless watermelon, chopped

2 cups/360 g cucumber, partially peeled, chopped

1 serrano pepper, minced

2 tbsp/3 g fresh mint, chopped

2 tbsp/30 ml fresh lime juice

3 tbsp/45 ml extra-virgin olive oil

¼ tsp sea salt

¼ tsp pepper

COOKING INSTRUCTIONS

Place red onion in a bowl and cover with filtered water and allow to sit for 10 minutes, while you chop the rest of the ingredients. Drain. Combine onion, watermelon, cucumber, pepper, mint, lime juice, olive oil, salt and pepper. Cover and chill in refrigerator for 1 hour to allow flavors to meld together.

COCONUT-LIME FRUIT SALAD

SERVES 6

The coconut-lime dressing adds a tropical feel to this lightly dressed fruit salad, a perfect addition to a summer brunch.

INGREDIENTS

2 cups/300 g strawberries, halved

2 cups/300 g honeydew melon, chopped into 1-inch/2-cm cubes

1 mango, chopped

¼ cup/60 ml coconut milk

4 tsp/20 ml fresh lime juice

2 tsp/1 g fresh basil, chopped

½ tsp raw honey

dash of sea salt

COOKING INSTRUCTIONS

Combine strawberries, honeydew and mango in a medium-sized bowl. In small bowl, whisk together coconut milk, lime juice, basil, honey and sea salt. Pour over fruit and serve.

FIG, PEAR AND PROSCIUTTO SALAD

SERVES 4

When you have the wonderful luck of pomegranate and fig seasons colliding, add pomegranate seeds to this tasty salad.

INGREDIENTS

2 pears, halved, seeded and cut lengthwise

Juice of 1 lemon

4 cups/750 g baby arugula

6 ripe figs, quartered

½ pomegranate with seeds removed (when in season)

8 slices prosciutto

FOR THE VINAIGRETTE:

3 tbsp/45 ml extra-virgin olive oil

2 tbsp/30 ml champagne vinegar

2 tbsp/30 ml balsamic vinegar

¼ tsp sea salt

¼ tsp pepper

1 tbsp fresh basil

COOKING INSTRUCTIONS

As soon as the pears are cut, squeeze fresh lemon juice on them to keep them from browning. Place 1 cup/185 g of arugula on each plate, top with pear, figs, pomegranate (if using) and 2 slices of prosciutto. Whisk together ingredients for vinaigrette and drizzle over salad.

TABBOULEH SALAD

SERVES 8

Tabbouleh is traditionally made with bulgur. The riced cauliflower is a perfect replacement, adding a hint of the light color associated with tabbouleh. Since parsley is the dominant flavor in tabbouleh, you don't miss much with this swap. This salad is also much easier to make when you don't have to prepare and soak the bulgur.

INGREDIENTS

2 cups/80 g packed parsley, chopped

1 cup/50 g green onion, chopped

1 cup/160 g tomato, seeds removed and diced

1 green bell pepper, diced

1 cup/230 g cauliflower, riced

2 tbsp/30 ml extra-virgin olive oil

2 tbsp/30 ml fresh lemon juice

½ tsp sea salt

¼ tsp pepper

COOKING INSTRUCTIONS

Gently combine all ingredients. Adjust salt, pepper and lemon juice to taste.

BUTTER-LETTUCE AND RADISH SALAD WITH GREEN GODDESS DRESSING

SERVES 4

Tahini, tangy lemon, creamy avocado and garlic combine to make a silky and delicious salad dressing. This is a thick and creamy dressing that pairs well with butter lettuce and savory prosciutto.

INGREDIENTS

FOR THE DRESSING (MAKES ABOUT 2 CUPS/472 ML):

1 cup/230 g avocado

2 cloves garlic

½ tsp lemon zest

¼ cup/60 ml, plus 1 tbsp/15 ml fresh lemon juice

2 tbsp/30 ml organic tahini

3 tbsp/45 ml extra-virgin olive oil

½ tsp sea salt

¼ tsp pepper

1 head butter lettuce, torn into pieces

8 small red radishes, sliced

1 scallion, roughly chopped

2 tbsp/5 g fresh parsley, roughly chopped

2 oz/60 g prosciutto, torn

COOKING INSTRUCTIONS

To make the dressing, combine all of the ingredients in a food processor and pulse until smooth. Mix all the ingredients for the salad in a large bowl. Separate salad onto plates. Top each salad with a couple of tablespoons of dressing and serve. Reserve remaining dressing for another use.

CURRIED CABBAGE SALAD

SERVES 6 TO 8

This curried salad is perfect for summer picnics and potlucks!

INGREDIENTS

1 red onion, very thinly sliced

filtered water

¼ cup/55 g Homemade Curried Mayonnaise (page 227)

2 tbsp/30 g almond butter

2 tbsp/20 g dried apricots

2 tbsp/3 g cilantro, chopped

2 tsp/10 g fresh ginger, minced

1 head cabbage, shredded

2 medium carrots, peeled and shredded

¼ cup/45 g slivered almonds

COOKING INSTRUCTIONS

Cover red onions with filtered water and let sit for 10 minutes to take out the bite. Drain. In a large bowl combine the mayo, almond butter, dried apricots, cilantro and ginger. Whisk until smooth. Add the cabbage, carrots and onion to the dressing and toss well to mix. Chill until needed. Garnish with slivered almonds.

SALAD SHIRAZI

SERVES 8

This is a traditional Persian salad, named after Shiraz, the town from which it originated. Salad Shirazi was a staple on the lunch and dinner table at my house growing up. Like many Middle Eastern foods, it is only lightly dressed, allowing the ingredients to shine. This simple salad can complement most dishes, and pairs particularly well with my Persian Herb Frittata (page 198).

INGREDIENTS

1 red onion, diced

filtered water

2 cups/320 g cucumber, chopped

2 cups/320 g tomatoes, chopped

¼ cup/10 g fresh parsley, chopped

2 tbsp/30 ml fresh lemon juice

1 ½ tbsp/25 ml extra-virgin olive oil

½ tsp sea salt

½ tsp pepper

COOKING INSTRUCTIONS

Place red onion in a bowl, cover with filtered water and allow to sit for 10 minutes while you chop the rest of the ingredients. Drain. Combine the red onion, cucumber, tomatoes, parsley, lemon juice, olive oil, salt and pepper.

THAI BEEF AND CUCUMBER SALAD

SERVES 4

This pungent, tangy and remarkably fresh salad makes a delicious and filling meal!

INGREDIENTS

FOR THE MARINADE:

1 ½ lbs/680 g flank steak

⅓ cup/80 ml coconut aminos

2 tbsp/30 ml lime juice

1 tbsp/15 g fresh ginger, minced

2 garlic cloves, crushed

½ tsp sea salt

FOR THE DRESSING:

3 tbsp/45 ml fresh lime juice

1 tbsp/15 ml fish sauce

1 tbsp/15 ml sesame oil (unrefined, expeller- or cold-pressed)

1 tbsp/15 ml coconut aminos

2 tsp/10 g fresh ginger, minced

1 clove garlic, minced

1 Thai hot pepper, minced

1 tsp/7 g raw honey

1 cup/130 g red onion, thinly sliced

filtered water

2 tbsp/30 ml expeller-pressed coconut oil

1 cup/160 g cucumber, peeled, sliced and halved

1 cup/160 g cherry tomatoes, halved

¼ cup/7 g fresh basil leaves, julienned

½ cup/15 g fresh cilantro leaves

COOKING INSTRUCTIONS

Cut beef into pieces about 1 ½ inches/4 cm long and ½ inch/1 cm wide. Combine beef marinade ingredients in large bowl. Add beef; toss to coat. Cover and marinate in refrigerator for at least 2 hours, up to overnight.

Whisk together dressing ingredients and set aside. Cover red onion with filtered water and let sit for 10 minutes to take out the bite. Remove steak from marinade; discard marinade. Heat coconut oil in large skillet over medium-high heat until hot. Add beef and stir-fry for 5 minutes, until it is lightly cooked through. If the pan is not large enough, do this in batches. Let the beef rest for 5–10 minutes and allow to cool. Toss onions, cucumber, tomatoes and dressing in a bowl. Mix to combine. Fold in basil and cilantro. Top with beef and serve.

CHEF'S TIP
I prefer expeller-pressed coconut oil for frying, as it has a subtler taste.

ROASTED BONE MARROW WITH ARUGULA AND PARSLEY SALAD

SERVES 4

Very little research has been conducted on the nutrition profile of bone marrow, but it is likely an excellent source of vitamin K and other fat-soluble vitamins. Besides being healthy, bone marrow has an incredible rich and creamy flavor that, in this salad, is brightened up with fresh herbs. It is surprisingly easy to make!

INGREDIENTS

8 3-4-inch/8-10 cm-long pieces marrow bones, preferably center cut

4 cups/720 g arugula

½ cup/20 g fresh flat-leaf parsley, roughly chopped

1 small shallot, thinly sliced

½ cucumber, peeled and sliced

½ cup/80 g cherry tomatoes, halved

2 tbsp/30 ml fresh lemon juice

1 tbsp/15 ml extra-virgin olive oil

sea salt and pepper

COOKING INSTRUCTIONS

Preheat oven to 450°F/232°C. Place marrow bones in a roasting pan, wider side down if they are uncut. If they are cut, cut side up. Roast bones until marrow is soft but before it begins to melt, about 15 to 20 minutes.

Meanwhile prepare the salad, tossing the arugula, parsley, shallot, cucumber, tomatoes, lemon juice and olive oil. Sprinkle with fresh sea salt and pepper.

Divide marrow bones among 4 plates, and serve with a side of salad. Use a long, thin spoon to scoop the marrow out if it is not center cut.

CHEF'S TIP
You can soak the shallots in water for 10 minutes to reduce the bite.

CRAB, PAPAYA AND CUCUMBER SALAD

SERVES 4

This is a perfect light and refreshing salad for a summer lunch!

INGREDIENTS

1 lb/455 g fresh crabmeat, picked through to remove small pieces of shell and cartilage

2 cups/360 g cucumber, peeled and chopped

4 cups/805 g papaya, chopped

1 serrano pepper, minced

1 tbsp/2 g cilantro, chopped

1 tbsp/2 g mint, chopped

FOR THE VINAIGRETTE:

2 tbsp/30 ml fresh orange juice

2 tbsp/30 ml fresh lime juice

1 tbsp/15 ml champagne vinegar

1 tbsp/15 ml extra-virgin olive oil

sea salt and pepper to taste

COOKING INSTRUCTIONS

In a large bowl, combine crabmeat, cucumber, papaya, serrano pepper, cilantro and mint. In a small bowl, whisk together orange juice, lime juice, champagne vinegar and olive oil to make the vinaigrette. Toss salad with vinaigrette. Adjust salt and pepper to taste.

CHEF'S TIP
Papayas are often genetically modified, either choose organic or verified GMO-free options.

Chapter 6

SOUPS & STEWS
for EVERY SEASON

Though soups can be comforting on a chilly winter night, I am going to show you how to include them as a staple all year round. My mom served *khoresht*, Persian stew, several nights of the week. Persian stews are made with liberal amounts of spice, giving the stews a unique flavor. You will find one of my favorites in this chapter. These are traditionally accompanied with basmati rice but, if you don't include rice in your diet, they are great alone or with cauliflower rice.

Soup is also a great way to use of all parts of the animal. The bones can be used to make broth, fish heads can be used to make soup and oxtail can be used to make stew. Most cultures around the world use many parts of the animal to make traditional soups. Armenians make a soup called *khash* using cows' feet, head and tripe. These parts of the animal are loaded with nutrients and flavor. If farmers can sell whole animals, not just premium cuts such as muscle meats, their farms will be more sustainable. It's a win-win for everyone!

Soups are so versatile. They can be a starter to an elegant dinner or be the star of the show themselves. Either way, they are tasty and chock-full of nutrients!

GARLIC SOUP WITH BROCCOLI RABE AND POACHED EGGS

SERVES 4

Most garlic and egg soup recipes I have seen call for day-old bread. By swapping out the bread for broccoli rabe, we end up with a more flavorful and nutritious meal. The slightly bitter and spicy flavor of the broccoli rabe pairs perfectly with the rich flavor of the runny egg yolk.

INGREDIENTS

2 tbsp/30 g ghee

1 medium onion, sliced

6 cloves garlic, chopped

6 cups/1440 ml Chicken Broth (page 202)

1 tsp/5 g sea salt

1 lb/454 g broccoli rabe, chopped

4 eggs

splash of white vinegar

fresh parsley (garnish)

COOKING INSTRUCTIONS

In a stockpot, heat ghee over medium heat. Cook the onion until soft and translucent, about 7 minutes. Add the garlic and cook until fragrant, about 1 minute. Add the chicken broth and salt and bring to a simmer. Reduce the heat and simmer for 15 minutes. Add the broccoli rabe and simmer for another 10 minutes.

Crack the eggs into 4 small bowls. Make sure the soup stays at a simmer. Add a splash of white vinegar to the soup. Slide the eggs into the soup and simmer until the whites are firm and the yolks are runny, about 4 minutes. Ladle a poached egg and some soup into each bowl, top with a sprig of parsley and serve.

CHEF'S TIP
When using white vinegar, choose organic or verified GMO-free. The starting ingredient is often corn, and if the corn isn't organic then there is a high chance of it being genetically modified (GMO).

CARAMELIZED ONION AND BEET SOUP

SERVES 6

The sweet and smoky caramelized onions paired with the earthy beets give this soup a rich and satisfying flavor that simultaneously evokes sophistication and comfort.

INGREDIENTS

2 lbs/907 g fresh beets, peeled and chopped

5 cups/1183 ml Chicken Broth (page 202)

½ tsp sea salt

¼ tsp pepper

2 tbsp/30 g butter

1 large onion, thinly sliced

1 carrot, peeled and diced

COOKING INSTRUCTIONS

Place the beets in a large stockpot. Add 4 cups/950 ml chicken broth, salt and pepper. Cover and cook for 45 minutes or until beets are tender. Meanwhile, heat the butter in a large skillet over medium heat. Sauté the onion and carrot, constantly stirring until carrots are tender and onion is soft, and they give off a sweet aroma. Once onion and carrots are soft, add them to the beets and broth. Let the soup cool a little bit, then transfer to a blender, add the additional broth and blend until smooth. Place the soup back into a pot and adjust salt and pepper to taste. Bring back to a simmer and serve.

WATERCRESS SOUP

SERVES 4

Watercress can be hard to come by, so I snatch it up whenever I see it to make this soup. The watercress adds the perfect amount of pepper and spice to an otherwise sweet soup.

INGREDIENTS

3-4 tbsp/44-60 g butter

1 cup/150 g yellow onions, finely chopped

4 cups/950 ml Chicken Broth (page 202)

1 medium sweet potato, peeled and diced

½ tsp sea salt

¼ tsp pepper

3 sprigs thyme

3 cups/540 g watercress

COOKING INSTRUCTIONS

Melt the butter in a heavy pot. Add the onions and sauté until translucent. Add the chicken broth, sweet potato, thyme, salt and pepper. Bring to a boil, reduce heat and simmer, partially covered, until sweet potato is very tender, about 20 minutes. Remove the thyme sprigs from the soup and discard.

Meanwhile, remove the leaves from the watercress and rinse. Add the watercress to the pot, cover, remove from heat and allow to cool. Put soup in a food processor and process until smooth. Return the soup to the pot and add more broth if it seems too thick. Adjust salt and pepper to taste and simmer until heated through.

CHEF'S TIP
I prefer Japanese sweet potato for this soup, as it is sweeter than most sweet potatoes.

HOPAR'S CHUNKY GAZPACHO

SERVES 8

When I was growing up, my *hopar* (Armenian for dad's brother) owned an Italian restaurant. I loved the gazpacho they served, so refreshing on hot Los Angeles summer nights. It truly hit the spot! I asked him for the recipe and he didn't remember the amounts, but he did remember all the ingredients. I experimented until I got it right!

INGREDIENTS

½ cup/40 g each red and green bell peppers, finely chopped

½ cup/120 g shallot, finely chopped

3 garlic cloves, finely chopped

½ cup/90 g cucumbers, peeled and finely chopped

2 tbsp/6 g scallions, finely chopped

6 tomatoes, peeled, seeded and diced (page 212)

3 cups/710 ml tomato juice

¼ cup/60 ml red wine vinegar

2 tbsp/30 ml extra-virgin olive oil

2 tbsp/5 g fresh dill, chopped

1 ½ tbsp/22 ml high-quality balsamic vinegar

1 tsp/5 g sea salt

COOKING INSTRUCTIONS

In a large bowl, combine bell peppers, shallot, garlic, cucumbers, scallions, tomatoes, tomato juice, red wine vinegar, olive oil and dill. Cover and refrigerate, preferably overnight. Add balsamic vinegar and salt and serve.

THAI-INSPIRED CHICKEN SOUP

SERVES 8

This Thai take on chicken soup is so refreshing that you can even enjoy it on a summer day! The homemade broth is a powerhouse full of easily digested nutrients, such as calcium and magnesium. It is also rich in collagen, gelatin and amino acids.

INGREDIENTS

1 stalk lemongrass, trimmed, peeled and chopped

8 cups/1.9 L Chicken Broth (page 202)

1 large shallot, chopped (about 1 cup/236 ml)

3 cloves garlic, chopped

1 tsp/5 g sea salt

3 kaffir lime leaves

1 2 inch/5 cm piece of fresh ginger, peeled and chopped

3 tbsp/45 ml fish sauce

1 ½ lbs/680 g boneless, skinless chicken thighs, thinly sliced about 2 inch/5 cm long and ½ inch/1 cm wide

2 Thai peppers, chopped

1 red bell pepper, sliced

2 cups/360 g zucchini (2 medium or 1 large), chopped in circles, then halved

1 cup/65 g shitake mushroom, sliced, stems removed if tough

½ cup/15 g fresh basil, julienned

2 tbsp/30 ml fresh lime juice

COOKING INSTRUCTIONS

Cut the top off the lemongrass, remove the tough outer layers and cut into 4 pieces. Heat chicken broth, lemongrass, shallot, garlic, salt, kaffir lime leaves, ginger and 2 tbsp/30 ml fish sauce in a heavy stockpot over medium-low heat. Bring to a light simmer, cover and cook for 30 minutes. Strain broth through a mesh sieve, discard solids and return broth back to the stockpot. Add the chicken, Thai peppers, bell pepper and zucchini. Simmer for 15 minutes. Add the shitake mushrooms and simmer for another 10 minutes. Turn off the heat. Add the basil, lime juice and additional tablespoon of fish sauce. Adjust seasoning to taste.

KHORESHT LUBIA SABZ (PERSIAN GREEN BEAN STEW)

SERVES 4

Unlike most Persian dishes, Khoresht Lubia Sabz is actually fairly simple to make. The traditional stew calls for diced tomatoes but my mom improvised with sun-dried tomatoes. We all preferred her new version!

INGREDIENTS

2 tbsp/30 g ghee

1 cup/150 g onion, diced

3 garlic cloves, minced

¼ tsp turmeric

1 lb/454 g stew meat, cut into 1-inch/2-cm cubes

½ tsp sea salt

¼ tsp pepper

2 tbsp/30 ml tomato paste

¼ cup/40 g sun-dried tomatoes, packed in olive oil, chopped

2 cups/470 ml Beef Broth (page 204)

1 lb/455 g green beans, stems removed and cut into 1 ½ inch/ 3.8 cm pieces

2 tbsp/30 ml fresh lemon juice

COOKING INSTRUCTIONS

Heat a skillet with a lid over medium-high heat. Add the ghee. Add the onion and cook until translucent, about 10 minutes. Add the garlic and turmeric and mix well. Season the meat with salt and pepper. Add to the skillet and brown on all sides. Add the tomato paste and sun-dried tomatoes, and mix well. Add the broth, cover and simmer on low for 1 hour. Add green beans and lemon juice and simmer for an additional 30 minutes uncovered, until green beans are soft but not soggy.

CURRIED CHICKEN AND BUTTERNUT SQUASH SOUP

SERVES 6

Butternut squash makes for a naturally sweet and luxuriously creamy soup. With the addition of diced chicken, the soup is surprisingly filling and can be served as a main course.

INGREDIENTS

4 tbsp/60 g butter

1 cup/150 g white onion, chopped

2 tbsp/15 g curry powder

1 large butternut squash, about
4-4 ½ cups/600-675 g chopped

1 whole chicken, quartered

3 cups/710 ml Chicken Broth
(page 202)

2 cups/475 ml coconut milk

sea salt and pepper to taste

chives, chopped (garnish)

COOKING INSTRUCTIONS

Melt the butter in a stockpot. Add the onion and curry powder, and cook until soft, about 10 minutes. Add the butternut squash, chicken and broth. Cover and cook on low heat until the vegetables are tender and the chicken is cooked through, about 45 minutes.

Cool chicken in the stock. Remove the meat from the bones and dice it. Pour the soup through a strainer. Put the solids into a blender with 1 cup/236 ml of the broth. Purée until smooth. Return puréed soup to the pot with the remaining liquid. Stir in coconut milk. Add diced chicken and simmer for 15 minutes. Add salt and pepper to taste. Garnish with chives.

KALE, SHITAKE MUSHROOM AND BEEF SOUP

SERVES 4

Soup is one of our favorite meals. We love the flexibility it offers, as our fridge is always filled with a variety of vegetables from local farms. Soup allows us to get creative in the kitchen and mix and match combinations. This soup is one of our favorites. With their earthy flavor, the mushrooms add the perfect richness and depth.

INGREDIENTS

½ cup/120 g shallots, chopped

2 tbsp/30 g ghee

1 ½ lb/455 g beef stew meat, cut into 1-inch/2-cm chunks

1 ½ cups/115 g shitake mushrooms, stems removed, chopped

1 carrot, peeled and diced

4 cloves garlic, minced

2 tomatoes, peeled and chopped

4 cups/950 ml Beef Broth (page 204)

1 tsp/5 g sea salt

½ tsp pepper

½ tsp red pepper flakes

1 bunch curly kale, stems removed and leaves chopped

1 tbsp/15 ml coconut aminos

COOKING INSTRUCTIONS

Heat a heavy-bottomed pot or Dutch oven over medium-high heat. Add ghee and shallots, and lightly sauté shallots until translucent, 5 to 7 minutes. Add the meat, stir and brown it on all sides, about 5 minutes. Set aside.

Add more ghee if needed. Add the chopped shitake mushrooms and cook for 3 to 5 minutes or until mushrooms are browned. Add carrots and garlic and sauté until fragrant, 1 to 2 minutes. Add tomatoes, beef broth, browned beef, salt, pepper and red pepper flakes. Bring to a simmer, then lower heat and cook for 30 minutes or until meat and vegetables are tender. Add kale and coconut aminos and cook for an additional 10 minutes or until kale is tender. Adjust salt and pepper to taste and serve!

SLOW-COOKER HAWAIIAN OXTAIL SOUP

SERVES 6 TO 8

Oxtail is a tough but flavorful cut of meat that becomes very tender when cooked slowly. This Hawaiian version of oxtail soup is thin and light. The toppings are reminiscent of a Vietnamese pho. Traditionally this soup calls for peanuts but due to their creamy nature, cashews are a perfect Paleo substitute.

Oxtail bones have a lot of collagen, which makes for a gelatinous stock. Gelatin has many benefits, including improving digestion and soothing the GI tract.

INGREDIENTS

3 lbs/1 kg oxtail

1 strip orange peel (zest, not the pith)

4 cloves garlic

3 star anise

2-inch/5-cm piece of fresh ginger, peeled

1 tbsp/15 g sea salt

½ cup/85 g cashews

filtered water

1 tbsp/15 ml apple cider vinegar

1 bunch mustard greens

¼ tsp chili pepper flakes

FOR GARNISH:

coconut aminos

fresh cilantro

scallions, chopped

fresh ginger, grated

COOKING INSTRUCTIONS

Place oxtail, orange peel, garlic cloves, star anise, ginger, salt and cashews in a slow cooker. Cover with filtered water. Add 1 tablespoon/15 ml of apple cider vinegar. Cook on low for 10 to 12 hours. Allow the soup to cool. Move to a stockpot with a lid and chill in the refrigerator overnight.

By the next day, the fat will have solidified. Pull the fat off the oxtail and remove the star anise, orange peel and ginger. Bring the soup to a simmer. Add the mustard greens and the chili pepper flakes. Cook for 7 to 10 minutes or until mustard greens are tender. The meat can either be stripped from the bones before serving or the oxtails can be served bone in. Serve with coconut aminos, fresh cilantro, chopped green onions and freshly grated ginger for garnish.

CHEF'S TIP
For best results, trim oxtail of any excess fat. Better yet, ask your butcher to trim it for you!

SLOW COOKER BEEF BURGUNDY

SERVES 6

Beef Burgundy, also know as Beef bourguignon, is an iconic French recipe. It is a sumptuous and comforting slow-cooked stew. It is delicious over mashed potatoes or cauliflower mash.

INGREDIENTS

6 pieces bacon, chopped

1 large onion, chopped

2 large carrots, peeled and chopped

4 cloves garlic, minced

2 tbsp/30 ml tomato paste, preferably in a glass jar

2½ lbs/1130 g beef stew meat or chuck roast, cut into 2-inch/5 cm cubes

salt and pepper

10 fresh thyme sprigs

1½ cups/350 ml Pinot Noir

2 cups/475 ml Beef Broth (bay leaves)

1 bay leaf

¼ cup fresh parsley leaves, minced for garnish

2 tbsp/30 g butter

1 cup/150 g of onions, sliced

8 oz/230 g of mushrooms, stems discarded and sliced

COOKING INSTRUCTIONS

Cook bacon until crisp, in a heavy bottom pot with a lid or a Dutch oven over medium-high heat. Remove the bacon from the pan with a slotted spoon and set aside. Pour bacon fat into a small bowl or a glass jar, leave enough behind to sauté the vegetables, about 1 tablespoon. Add chopped onion and carrots to the skillet and sauté until soft, about 5 to 7 minutes, add garlic cloves and sauté until fragrant about 1 minute. Transfer the vegetables to a bowl and set aside. Generously add salt and pepper to the beef. Add another tablespoon of bacon fat if needed to the pot. Brown the beef, turning to make sure all sides are browned, about 7 minutes. Add the tomato paste, stirring frequently to make sure beef is well coated and cook until tomato paste goes from a bright red to a brick color, about 45 seconds. Add the wine, and use a wooden spoon to scrape up any brown bits from the bottom of your pot. Add the broth, bay leaves, and thyme. Cover the pot with a lid and turn the heat down to low. Cook for 1½ hours covered. Cook for an additional 30 minutes uncovered to allow the sauce to thicken. Discard thyme sprigs and bay leaves. 15 minutes before the beef is ready, prep the sliced onions and mushrooms for garnish. Add butter to a medium-sized saucepan and turn heat to medium. Add onions and sauté for 5 minutes, add mushrooms and sauté for an additional 10 minutes, or until onions and mushrooms are tender. Add cooked and chopped bacon back to the beef. Adjust salt and pepper of beef to taste. Garnish with chopped parsley and mushroom and onion sauté and serve.

Chapter 7

Delectable
SIDE DISHES

Side dishes not only add a variety of micronutrients to a healthy diet, they liven up the dinner table with color and flavor. Ever since I adopted a Paleo diet, the range of vegetables I cook has tremendously widened. I become ecstatic at the sight of something I have never tried or made before. A CSA is a great way to broaden your veggie horizons!

I have included a variety of sides here that can be prepared quickly to accompany many of your favorite main dishes.

PEPPER AND CARROT PURÉE

SERVES 4

My husband thinks this is the best side dish that I have ever made and I think I agree! Serve with my Sun-Dried-Tomato-and-Fennel-Braised Short Ribs (page 75) or my Panfried Filet with Shallot Sauce (page 71).

INGREDIENTS

2 red bell peppers, halved and seeded

1 ½ lbs/680 g carrots, peeled and chopped

2 tbsp/30 ml balsamic vinegar

½ tsp sea salt

¼ tsp pepper

¼ cup/60 g butter

½ tsp sweet paprika

2 tbsp/5 g cilantro

COOKING INSTRUCTIONS

Preheat oven to 350°F/177°C. Place peppers on a baking sheet, cut-side down. Bake for 45 minutes or until peppers are blackened. Remove the skins. While the peppers are baking, place carrots in a large pot, cover with water and bring to a boil. Boil until carrots are soft, about 30–45 minutes. Drain carrots. Using an immersion blender purée the peppers, carrots, balsamic vinegar, salt, pepper, butter, paprika and cilantro.

BRAISED SAVOY CABBAGE

SERVES 4

We often receive savoy cabbage from our CSA. This is one of my favorite ways to prepare it. The cabbage and carrots become sweeter as they cook, and the addition of bacon makes this a perfect marriage between sweet and savory. This is excellent served with my Citrus-Braised Pork Shoulder (page 94).

INGREDIENTS

4 bacon slices, diced

1 head cabbage

1 cup/200 g carrots, peeled and diced

½ yellow onion, diced

¼ cup/40 g green garlic, diced

sea salt and pepper

½ cup/120 ml Chicken Broth (page 204)

COOKING INSTRUCTIONS

Heat a heavy-bottomed pan over medium-low heat. Add bacon and cook until crispy. Once bacon is cooked, set bacon bits aside, leaving bacon fat in the pan. Let the bacon fat cool slightly.

Meanwhile, cut the heads of the cabbage in quarters. Cut out the cores and cut the quarters into thick slices. Add the carrots and onion to the pan and cook over medium-high heat until soft, about 10 minutes. Add the garlic and sauté for 2 more minutes. Stir in the cabbage and generously salt and pepper. Add the chicken broth. Turn down the heat to a simmer, cover and cook for about 15 minutes or more until the cabbage is tender and chicken broth has evaporated. Top with bacon bits and serve immediately.

HONEY-AND-CITRUS-GLAZED PARSNIPS

SERVES 4

These parsnips will likely be devoured straight from the baking dish. Roasting them with honey plays up their sweetness and the citrus offers the perfect tang. These parsnips are a perfect accompaniment to my Pork Chops with Pomegranate-Ginger Sauce (page 93).

INGREDIENTS

FOR THE GLAZE:

juice of half an orange

juice of half a lime

2 tbsp/45 g raw honey

6 parsnips, peeled, trimmed and cut into batons

sea salt and pepper

leaves from 3 sprigs thyme

3 tbsp/45 ml coconut oil or ghee

COOKING INSTRUCTIONS

Preheat the oven to 350°F/177°C. Mix the orange juice, lime juice and honey. Place the parsnips in an ovenproof dish or baking sheet. Season parsnips generously with salt and pepper, add thyme and drizzle with $\frac{2}{3}$ of your glaze. Toss the parsnips with the melted ghee or coconut oil. Cook for 20 minutes. Add the rest of the glaze and toss to make sure the parsnips are well combined. Cook for an additional 20 minutes or until the parsnips are soft and lightly browned.

CUMIN-ROASTED CARROTS

SERVES 6

The pungent, earthy aroma of cumin combined with a hint of sweetness from the orange make this dish delightful. These carrots are delicious served with my Tandoori Chicken (page 87).

INGREDIENTS

¼ tsp sea salt

1 ½ tsp/4 g cumin

¼ tsp coriander

3 tbsp/45 ml fresh orange juice

zest of 1 orange

1 tsp/1 g fresh thyme

2 lbs/910 g carrots, peeled whole

2 cloves garlic, minced

3 tbsp/45 ml ghee, melted

COOKING INSTRUCTIONS

Preheat oven to 400°F/204°C. Mix the salt, cumin, coriander, orange juice, orange zest and thyme in a bowl. Reserve 2 tbsp/30 ml of mixture. Spread carrots and garlic on a baking sheet, toss with ghee and drizzle with sauce. Make sure it is well combined. Bake for 30 minutes or until carrots are tender. Toss with remaining sauce and serve.

WHOLE ROASTED SWEET POTATOES WITH TWO TOPPINGS

I first offered this to accommodate picky guests. Now every time I serve these potatoes, most people have 2 servings, as they can't decide which topping they prefer! We love this paired with my Flank Steak with Cilantro Sauce (page 65). The ingredients below make enough dressing to cover approximately 12 sweet potatoes.

INGREDIENTS

FOR TOPPING 1:

¼ cup/60 ml extra-virgin olive oil

1 tsp/1 g fresh rosemary, minced

2 cloves garlic, minced

Top with Crispy Sage (page 213)

FOR TOPPING 2:

3 tbsp/45 ml coconut oil

½ tsp ground cinnamon

⅛ tsp ground nutmeg

COOKING INSTRUCTIONS

Preheat oven to 400°F/204°C. Prick each sweet potato a few times with a fork. Place them on a baking tray on the top rack of an oven and cook for 50–60 minutes or until they are completely tender.

Meanwhile, prep your toppings by whisking together the ingredients for each option. Serve alongside roasted sweet potatoes and allow your guests to pick their own toppings!

ROASTED PARSNIPS AND APPLES

SERVES 6

This combination of roasted apples and parsnips is the perfect accompaniment to my Slow-Cooked Macadamia Rosemary Salmon (page 113).

INGREDIENTS

1 ½ lbs/680 g parsnips, peeled and chopped

2 large apples, cored and chopped

1 medium shallot, chopped (about ½ cup/160 g)

1 tbsp/3 g fresh sage, chopped, plus 1 tsp/1 g fresh sage, chopped

¼ cup/60 ml ghee, melted

½ tsp sea salt

¼ tsp pepper

1 tbsp/15 ml fresh orange juice

1 tsp/5 g orange zest

COOKING INSTRUCTIONS

Preheat oven to 425°F/218°C. Combine parsnips, apples, shallots, 1 tbsp/3 g sage, ghee, salt and pepper. Toss to combine and spread onto a baking sheet. Cook for 1 hour. Halfway through, open oven and toss the ingredients to make sure the fruit and vegetables are well combined. After cooking, toss with orange juice, orange zest and additional teaspoon/1 g of sage. Serve.

BABY ZUCCHINI WITH FRESH GARDEN HERBS

SERVES 4

When zucchini season rolls around, my fridge is usually overflowing, between the farmers' market and the generosity of gardening friends. I am always looking for new ways to prepare zucchini, but this simple sautéed version with fresh herbs remains my favorite. You can serve these with just about anything, but they are especially tasty with my Grape Leaf and Cabbage Dolmas (page 76).

INGREDIENTS

1 tbsp/15 ml ghee

1 ½ lbs/680 g baby zucchini, chopped in ½-inch/1-cm coins

sea salt and pepper

1 tsp/1 g fresh oregano, chopped

1 tbsp/3 g fresh parsley, chopped

COOKING INSTRUCTIONS

Heat ghee in a heavy-bottomed skillet with a lid. Add zucchinis and season with salt and pepper. Put lid on and cook for 5 minutes. Cook for an additional 5 minutes uncovered. Sprinkle with fresh herbs. Adjust salt and pepper to taste.

CHORIZO CAULIFLOWER RICE

SERVES 4

This dish bursts with flavor, and can be served as a side or a one-pot meal. The chorizo adds heat and makes this dish rich and satisfying.

INGREDIENTS

1 head cauliflower

1 tbsp/15 ml ghee

½ large red onion, diced

1 red bell pepper, chopped

3 cloves garlic, minced

½ lb/230 g chorizo

1 tsp/1 g smoked paprika

1 tsp/1 g dried red pepper flakes

¼ cup/60 ml Chicken Broth (page 202)

cilantro, chopped and avocado, sliced (garnish)

COOKING INSTRUCTIONS

Remove the stem of the cauliflower and put through food processor until it resembles rice. Heat ghee over medium-high heat in a heavy-bottomed pan. Sauté onions and bell pepper until soft, about 5 minutes. Add garlic and chorizo. Sauté for a few minutes, until chorizo starts to lightly brown. Then add cauliflower, paprika and red pepper flakes. Sauté for a minute or two, until all the ingredients are well combined. Add chicken broth and cook until cauliflower is tender and broth has evaporated. Serve topped with cilantro and sliced avocado.

BRAISED RED CABBAGE WITH FENNEL AND APPLE

SERVES 4

This aromatic dish is the perfect accompaniment to roasted or pan-fried fish. Try it with my Panfried Cod with Herb Sauce (page 115).

INGREDIENTS

2 tbsp/30 ml butter

1 small white onion, chopped

2 fennel bulbs, sliced

2 apples, cored and chopped

2 cloves garlic, minced

½ head of purple cabbage, chopped

½ cup/120 ml Chicken Broth (page 202)

Sea salt and pepper

COOKING INSTRUCTIONS

Heat butter in a large sauté pan over medium heat. Add onion, fennel and apple and sauté until soft, about 10 minutes. Add garlic and cook for an additional minute, until fragrant. Add cabbage and broth. Generously salt and pepper. Toss to make sure it is all well coated and well mixed. Turn the heat to low and let cook until cabbage is tender, about 25 minutes. Adjust salt and pepper and serve.

SAUTÉED BROCCOLI WITH PARSLEY AND ANCHOVY SAUCE

SERVES 4

The anchovies combined with butter impart a perfectly savory flavor, or umami, to the broccoli. This dish is excellent with a lightly seasoned grilled meat.

INGREDIENTS

1 lb/455 g broccoli rabe, ends trimmed

¾ cup/180 ml water

1 tbsp/15 g butter

2 cloves garlic, minced

FOR THE SAUCE:

3 anchovy fillets, minced

1 tbsp/15 ml extra-virgin olive oil

½ tsp lemon zest

1 tbsp/3 g fresh flat-leaf parsley, chopped

½ tsp crushed red pepper

¼ tsp sea salt

COOKING INSTRUCTIONS

Place water in a large skillet with broccoli rabe and heat over medium-low heat. Cover and allow it to steam, about 8–10 minutes. When the water has evaporated and the broccoli is fairly tender remove the cover and add butter and garlic. Sauté for 3 minutes until broccoli is lightly browned. In a separate bowl, mix anchovies, olive oil, lemon zest, parsley, red pepper and salt. Pour sauce over broccoli rabe. Toss and serve.

CAULIFLOWER AND LEEK MASH

SERVES 4

Cauliflower mash pairs well with almost any protein, but it's particularly good with Beef Cheek Braised with Tomatoes (page 66).

INGREDIENTS

1 small head cauliflower, cut into florets

1 cup/240 ml Chicken Broth (page 202)

3 pieces of bacon, diced

¼ cup/45 g leeks, thinly sliced

3 cloves garlic, minced

1-2 tbsp/15-30 g butter

¼ cup/10 g fresh parsley, chopped

COOKING INSTRUCTIONS

Place cauliflower and chicken broth in a pot with a tight-fitting lid. Bring to a boil, then simmer until cauliflower is tender and mashes easily.

Meanwhile, heat a heavy-bottomed pan over medium-low heat. Add bacon and cook until crispy. Once bacon is cooked, set bacon bits aside, leaving bacon fat in the pan. Let the bacon fat cool slightly.

While cauliflower is cooking, add leeks to the bacon grease and sauté over medium heat. Sauté leeks until soft, about 5 minutes. Add garlic and sauté for a minute or two until fragrant. Set aside. Once cauliflower is ready, mash down with a fork and add leek/garlic sauté and butter to pot. Use 2 tbsp/30 g of butter, if you prefer a creamier consistency. Use an immersion blender to thoroughly mix to desired consistency. Mix in chopped parsley with a fork. Top with bacon and serve!

BLACK SESAME GREEN BEANS

SERVES 4

Although you can use any color sesame seeds, the black gives this dish an elegant feel. These green beans pair well with Macadamia-Crusted Duck Breast with Spicy "Soy" Ginger Sauce (page 88).

INGREDIENTS

2 tbsp/30 ml coconut oil, preferably expeller-pressed

1 lb/455 g green beans, ends trimmed

1 tbsp/15 ml coconut aminos

1 tsp/5 ml unrefined, expeller- or cold-pressed sesame oil

1 tbsp/10 g toasted black sesame seeds

sea salt and pepper to taste

COOKING INSTRUCTIONS

Heat coconut oil in a wok or heavy-bottomed skillet over medium-high heat. Add green beans and sauté until tender, about 7 to 10 minutes. Turn off heat, add coconut aminos, sesame oil and sesame seeds. Add salt and pepper to taste.

BUTTER-BRAISED RADISHES

SERVES 4

These radishes are tender, peppery and slightly sweet. The flavor is mild enough that they can be enjoyed alongside most entrees, but they are particular good with Panfried Filet with Shallot Sauce (page 71).

INGREDIENTS

2 cups/400 g radishes, sliced and tops removed

2 tbsp/30 ml unsalted butter

¼ cup/60 g shallots, finely chopped

½ cup/120 ml Chicken Broth (page 202)

2 tsp/10 ml apple cider vinegar

2 tsp/15 g raw honey

¼ tsp sea salt

dash of pepper

COOKING INSTRUCTIONS

Trim the radishes and slice them into ⅓-inch/¾-cm thick rounds. Melt the butter over medium heat. Add the shallots and cook, stirring until soft. Add the radishes and cook, stirring occasionally until they begin to soften, 5 to 7 minutes. Add the broth. Bring to a simmer, cover and cook until the radishes are crisp but tender. Uncover, raise the heat to high and add the vinegar, honey and salt. Cook, stirring occasionally, until most of the liquid has evaporated to a glaze, 2 to 3 minutes. Sprinkle with a dash of pepper and serve immediately.

CARAMELIZED FENNEL

SERVES 4

When fennel cooks, the strong licorice or anise flavor tends to subside and, as it caramelizes, the fennel takes on a sweeter flavor. This is the perfect accompaniment to grilled fish or chicken.

INGREDIENTS

2 tbsp/30 g butter

2 medium fennel bulbs, halved and thinly sliced

½ tsp sea salt

1 tbsp/15 ml balsamic vinegar

COOKING INSTRUCTIONS

Heat butter in a large skillet over medium heat. Add fennel and cook, stirring occasionally, until soft and beginning to brown, about 10 to 12 minutes. Sprinkle with salt, stir in vinegar and remove from heat.

CHEF'S TIP
Save the feathery fronds (tops of the fennel) and chop them up to add flavor to soups and salads.

SPICED CHARD WITH CURRANTS

SERVES 4

This slightly sweet and spicy side dish is delicious and quick to make. Try it with my Lamb Shanks with Apricots (page 101).

INGREDIENTS

2 tbsp/30 g ghee

½ cup/120 g shallots, minced

2 cloves garlic, minced

1 bunch red chard, stems removed and leaves julienned

½ tsp sea salt

¼ cup/60 g currants

1 tsp/5 g crushed red pepper flakes

1 cup/240 ml Chicken Broth (page 202) or water

COOKING INSTRUCTIONS

In a large skillet, heat ghee over medium heat. Add the shallots and cook, stirring, until soft, about 5 minutes. Add garlic and cook until fragrant, about 2 minutes. Take care so the garlic doesn't burn. Add chard, salt, currants and red pepper flakes. Stir and make sure it is all well mixed. Add broth or water and bring to a boil. Reduce heat to low and simmer for 15 to 20 minutes or until the liquid has evaporated. Stir occasionally. Taste and adjust salt as needed.

SHREDDED BRUSSELS SPROUTS WITH PANCETTA

SERVES 6

Salty and savory pancetta and nutty Brussels sprouts are a perfect pairing. This dish is delicious served with Balsamic Rosemary Roasted Chicken and Yams (page 78).

INGREDIENTS

1 ½ lbs/680 g Brussels sprouts

1 tbsp/15 g ghee

4 oz/115 g pancetta, diced

1 medium shallot, diced (about ½ cup/160 g)

2 cloves garlic, minced

¼ tsp sea salt

¼ tsp pepper

½ cup/120 ml Chicken Broth (page 202)

COOKING INSTRUCTIONS

Discard the stem end of the Brussels sprouts and use a food processor to shred the sprouts. Warm the ghee in a heavy-bottomed pan over medium-high heat. Add the pancetta and sauté until crisp. Add shallot and cook for a few minutes until soft, then add garlic and sauté for a minute until fragrant. Add the Brussels sprouts, salt, pepper and broth. Sauté until sprouts are soft and broth has reduced. Adjust salt and pepper and serve immediately.

ROASTED MEDITERRANEAN VEGETABLES

SERVES 6

This colorful and versatile vegetable medley can be served with many main courses, and is particularly tasty alongside Sun-Dried-Tomato-and-Fennel-Braised Short Ribs (page 75).

INGREDIENTS

2 large zucchinis, cut lengthwise then chopped

1 large eggplant, peeled and chopped

1 red bell pepper, seeded and chopped

1 red onion, chopped

5 medium tomatoes, whole

10 cloves garlic, whole

sea salt and pepper

2 tbsp/30 g ghee, melted

1 tbsp/15 ml balsamic vinegar

COOKING INSTRUCTIONS

Preheat oven to 375°F/190°C. Arrange zucchinis, eggplant, red bell pepper, red onion, tomatoes and garlic on a baking dish in a single layer. Generously salt and pepper the vegetables and toss them with melted ghee. Drizzle with balsamic vinegar. Cook for 25 minutes.

KUKU SABZI (PERSIAN HERB FRITTATA)

SERVES 6

There are many variations of *kuku sabzi*. Some include walnuts and dried barberries. The only version I ever knew growing up was the one my mom and aunts made. Their version is a simple one with lots of fresh herbs, eggs, salt and pepper. This dish is often served alongside lunch or dinner, but I also think it makes a great breakfast!

INGREDIENTS

3 bunches parsley

2 bunches cilantro

1 bunch dill

1 ½ cups/270 g leeks (light parts only), sliced

6 eggs

1 tsp/5 g sea salt

½ tsp pepper

3 tbsp/45 g ghee

COOKING INSTRUCTIONS

Wash and thoroughly dry your parsley, cilantro and dill. One they are washed and dried, pulse them in the food processor along with the leeks to chop them, but take care to not overblend them and make them soggy.

Crack the eggs in a separate bowl, add the salt and pepper and mix together. Combine the egg mixture with the herb mixture. Heat a heavy-bottomed pan such as cast iron over medium-low heat and add the ghee. Add the herb and egg mixture and cook until the edges are browned.

Watch your frittata carefully to make sure it cooks through but doesn't burn. Turn down heat if needed. Cooking it at a low temp the frittata may not be ready to flip for 30 minutes. Periodically run a spatula along the edges to loosen it, so it will flip more easily. Once ready, flip. My mom always flips the frittata whole. If you are finding that difficult, use your spatula to cut it into 4 pieces and flip each piece individually. Cook for another 10 minutes, until the other side is also browned and the frittata is cooked.

COCONUT CAULIFLOWER RICE

SERVES 4

This coconut cauliflower rice is the perfect accompaniment to my Bangkok Meatballs (page 58) or Steamed Salmon with Curried Pear and Mango Chutney (page 114).

INGREDIENTS

1 small head cauliflower

2 tbsp/30 ml coconut oil

¼ cup/15 g scallions, chopped

2 cloves garlic, minced

¼ cup/20 g shredded coconut

½ cup/120 ml coconut milk

¼ tsp sea salt

¼ tsp pepper

COOKING INSTRUCTIONS

Remove the stem of the cauliflower and put through food processor until it resembles rice. Heat coconut oil in a heavy-bottomed pan over medium heat. Sauté scallions for about 3 minutes, then add garlic and shredded coconut and sauté for an additional 3 minutes. Add milk and cauliflower rice. Stir occasionally to prevent it from sticking. Cook until liquid evaporates. Add salt and pepper to taste and serve.

Chapter 8

SAUCES & SALSAS
from Scratch

Making your own sauces, bases and condiments is more rewarding than buying them, and results in healthier dishes packed with flavor. Homemade broth gives soups and sauces depth and complexity that cannot be achieved with store-bought varieties. Homemade salad dressings made with fresh herbs and fresh oils are aromatic, have phenomenal flavor and lack the sugar that you often find in pre-packaged varieties.

A homemade stock, or broth, is the foundation of most well-prepared entrees and is essential for good home cooking. Homemade bone broth is one of the most nutrient-dense foods, rich in collagen, amino acids, gelatin and many minerals. The form calcium takes in bone broth is very easy for the body to absorb and digest. Research and observation of traditional cultures that cook with bones has taught us that gelatin has many benefits, including improving digestion and soothing the gastro intestinal tract. In addition, gelatin has been found to build strong cartilage and bones and also benefits the skin, immune system and heart. Gelatin and bone broth are true superfoods!

Most sauces, salsas, salad dressings and mayonnaise are simple to create at home. When making these items from scratch, you avoid questionable ingredients such as preservatives, vegetable oils and high-fructose corn syrup that are found in many store-bought varieties.

Whipping up sauces and salsas from scratch may take a few extra minutes, but you will be rewarded with a more delicious and healthier meal. Well worth the effort!

CHICKEN BROTH

MAKES 10–12 CUPS/2400–2840 ML

Although the heads and feet are listed as optional, I highly recommend that you include them when making broth, as these are the most gelatinous parts of the animal. Chicken skin is rich in collagen, and also a great addition to broth.

If you don't have all the vegetables on hand, just skip them. Each adds more depth and flavor to broth, but no one vegetable is necessary. The only three ingredients that are necessary are the bones, water and vinegar!

INGREDIENTS

3 lbs/1 kg chicken pieces (carcass, including necks and backs)

2 chicken heads (optional)

4 chicken feet (optional)

1 leek, cut into several pieces (white and green parts)

1 large onion quartered

2 carrots, peeled and cut in half

2 ribs celery, cut in half

2 bay leaves

10 sprigs parsley

8–12 cups/2–3 L filtered water

1 tbsp/15 ml apple cider vinegar

COOKING INSTRUCTIONS

Place the bones, chicken heads and feet (if using) in the slow cooker. Add the vegetables, bay leaves, water and apple cider vinegar. Cook on low for 10–12 hours. Remove all vegetables and bones and put broth through a strainer. Refrigerate overnight. The fat will have solidified at the top by the next day. Remove fat and discard or reserve for another use. Discard bay leaves. Refrigerate broth and use within a few days or freeze.

CHEF'S TIP
Make broth using a whole chicken. Allow broth to cool, remove meat from the carcass and use it for chicken salad or casseroles.

BEEF BROTH

MAKES 10–12 CUPS/2400–2840 ML

Adding roasted bones and vegetables to broth makes it more aromatic and flavorful. If you are in a hurry, throw your bones in to the slow cooker with filtered water and apple cider vinegar. You will still make a nutritious broth that will be much more flavorful than any store-bought variety. When you do have the time, I recommend taking the extra steps.

INGREDIENTS

4 lbs/2 kg beef bones

1 medium onion, quartered

2 carrots, peeled and cut in half

2 stalks celery, cut in half

4 sprigs thyme

1 bay leaf

8–12 cups/2–3 L filtered water

1 tbsp/15 ml apple cider vinegar

COOKING INSTRUCTIONS

Preheat oven to 450°F/232°C. Place the bones in a roasting pan and roast uncovered for 30 minutes. Transfer the bones to the slow cooker. Add the vegetables, thyme, bay leaf, water and apple cider vinegar. Cook on low for 8–24 hours. Remove all vegetables and bones, and put broth through a strainer. Refrigerate overnight. The fat will have solidified by the next day; remove it and discard or reserve for another use. Discard thyme and bay leaf. Refrigerate broth and use within a few days or freeze.

CHEF'S TIP

Freeze some broth in wide-mouth mason jars to use for soup. Freeze some in muffin tins and, once frozen, transfer to a plastic bag and store in freezer. These ½ cup/120-ml portions are the perfect slow-cooker recipes!

HOMEMADE KETCHUP

MAKES 2 CUPS/470 ML

Homemade ketchup isn't for everyone. Some of us are more attached to the familiar taste of store-bought ketchup. For me, store-bought ketchup was always too sweet, even more so since I'm eating Paleo.

This ketchup is light, sweet, tangy and has depth.

INGREDIENTS

2 tbsp/30 g ghee

1 cup/150 g onions, diced

1 tbsp/10 g garlic, minced

¼ bunch thyme, tied with kitchen string

3 lbs/1 kg tomatoes, peeled, seeded and diced (page 212)

¼ cup/60 ml maple syrup

⅓ cup/80 ml apple cider vinegar

¼ cup/60 ml tomato paste

1 bay leaf

½ tsp dry mustard powder

⅛ tsp cayenne

¼ tsp allspice

⅛ tsp crushed red pepper

2 tsp/10 g sea salt

COOKING INSTRUCTIONS

Heat a large skillet over medium-high heat. Add the ghee. Brown onions until soft, about 5 minutes. Add the garlic and sauté for 1 minute. Add the remaining ingredients. Bring to a boil, then simmer for 40 minutes, until slightly thickened.

Discard the thyme. Allow the sauce to cool and either purée with an immersion blender or transfer to a regular blender and purée until smooth. Return the ketchup to the pan and simmer for 1 hour, stirring occasionally. If stored in an airtight container, the ketchup can be kept in the fridge for up to a month.

CHEF'S TIP
Your ketchup will be as good as your tomatoes! It's best to make this recipe with organic tomatoes when they are in season.

HOMEMADE COCONUT MILK (THE EASY WAY)

MAKES 3-4 CUPS/700-950 ML

We try to limit our use of canned coconut milk. You can find some BPA-free brands, but most of them have additional ingredients such as guar gum. I still think the healthiest option is to make it yourself!

You can make coconut milk using various methods, including making it from desiccated coconuts or from fresh coconuts. The latter takes a fair amount of work. This method relies on a store-bought package of shredded coconut.

INGREDIENTS

8 oz/227 g package of finely shredded coconut

3-4 cups/700-950 ml of hot water, not boiling

COOKING INSTRUCTIONS

Place coconut and hot water in blender for about 45 seconds. Line a strainer with 2 layers of cheesecloth or use a nut milk bag. Pour the contents of the blender through the strainer and into a large bowl. Pull the edges of the cheesecloth together and squeeze out the remainder of the coconut milk. Refrigerate the coconut milk and use within 1-2 days.

CHEF'S TIP
Depending on your need, vary the amount of water. Less water will give you a creamier coconut milk. If you are making the milk to add to smoothies or a recipe that doesn't require a lot of cream, use more water and make more milk from one package. Coconut milk freezes well in freezer-safe glass jars!

PISTACHIO PESTO

MAKES ABOUT 2 CUPS/470 ML

Pesto is so versatile: herbs and nuts can be mixed and matched to provide endless flavor options.
I have yet to meet a pesto that I didn't like, at least just a little bit!

Pistachios replace the traditional pine nut in this pesto recipe, adding depth to the flavor.
Bonus: They are more affordable than pine nuts.

INGREDIENTS

1 ½ cups/40 g fresh basil

½ cup/20 g fresh parsley

1 tbsp/3 g fresh mint

¾ cup/125 g dry-roasted
pistachios, shelled

1 clove garlic

¼ cup/60 ml fresh lemon juice

½ tsp lemon zest

½ tsp sea salt

¼ tsp pepper

¾ cup/180 ml extra-virgin olive oil

COOKING INSTRUCTIONS

Combine basil, parsley, mint, pistachios, garlic, lemon juice, lemon zest, salt
and pepper in a food processor until coarsely chopped. Add the oil and
process until fully incorporated and smooth. Adjust salt and pepper to taste.

CHEF'S TIP
Pistachio pesto is excellent with eggs, added to lettuce wraps or served
with zucchini noodles and my Lemon-Garlic Chicken (page 82).

FOUR-HERB SPICY CHIMICHURRI

MAKES ABOUT 2 CUPS/470 ML

Chimichurri is an Argentinian sauce typically served with grilled meats. I first had it in 2004 when I visited Argentina, and later again when I spotted a recipe. I have been making many variations since. This four-herb version is my favorite.

INGREDIENTS

1 cup/40 g fresh parsley

½ cup/20 g fresh cilantro

¼ cup/10 g fresh basil

1 tbsp/3 g oregano

2 tbsp/20 g white onion, chopped

2 tbsp/20 g red bell pepper chopped

1 serrano pepper, chopped

3 cloves garlic

½ tsp sea salt

½ tsp pepper

½ tsp cumin

1 tsp/7 g chili powder

6 tbsp/90 ml extra-virgin olive oil

2 tbsp/30 ml red wine vinegar

COOKING INSTRUCTIONS

Mix all ingredients in a food processor. Pulse a few times until blended but still coarse.

CHEF'S TIP
The chimichurri can be served immediately, but the flavors are greatly improved after a few hours.

BLANCHING AND PEELING TOMATOES

I rarely use canned tomatoes, as I can easily cut, peel and chop them myself! Blanching tomatoes is healthier and less wasteful than buying canned, as you minimize your use of packaging!

INGREDIENTS

up to 8 tomatoes per round of blanching

COOKING INSTRUCTIONS

Boil about 4 quarts of water. Set up a cold-water bath by placing water and ice cubes in a large bowl. Cut an "x" in the bottom of each tomato, carefully drop in the boiling water and cook for 1 minute or until skin starts to break. Remove a few tomatoes at a time and dunk in the cold bath. You should be able to easily peel the skin off by hand. Peel the skin, cut the tomatoes in half and scoop or squeeze the seeds out. Use as needed.

CRISPY SAGE

SERVES 8

Delicate and crunchy with a wonderfully piney flavor, crispy sage adds an impressive touch to burgers or roasted sweet potatoes.

INGREDIENTS

1 bunch fresh sage

3 tbsp/45 g butter

coarse sea salt

COOKING INSTRUCTIONS

Pinch off leaves from sage. Heat butter in a medium-sized skillet over medium-high heat until hot. Watch closely so as not to burn. Fry the sage leaves in batches, taking care not to overcrowd the pan. Place them stem-side up and cook for 30 seconds each until crispy and very lightly browned. Transfer to a paper towel and sprinkle with sea salt.

CHIPOTLE PEPPERS IN ADOBO SAUCE

MAKES ABOUT 2 CUPS OR 7–10 PEPPERS

Chipotle peppers in adobo sauce are one of my favorite ingredients. They add smoky heat and depth to otherwise simple dishes such as fruit salsa.

I stopped using them when I started following a Paleo diet, as many of the canned varieties are loaded with questionable ingredients. I finally made my own recipe that tastes identical to the store-bought version.

INGREDIENTS

7-10 chipotle peppers, stems removed and split lengthwise

1 cup/160 g strained tomatoes in a jar

1 cup/240 ml Beef Broth (page 204)

¼ cup/60 ml apple cider vinegar

¼ cup/40 g onion, minced

2 cloves garlic, crushed

2 tbsp/45 g raw honey

½ tsp sea salt

½ tsp cumin

¼ tsp cinnamon

⅛ tsp allspice

pinch of cloves

COOKING INSTRUCTIONS

Combine all of the ingredients in a pan, bring to a simmer, cover and simmer on low for 30 minutes. Remove the lid and simmer on low for an additional 30 minutes to allow the sauce to thicken. Once the sauce has thickened, cool sauce and peppers and store for later use. They should keep in the fridge for about a week, or you can freeze them for later use.

CHEF'S TIP
Freeze these in ice-cube trays and use as needed.

GHEE

MAKES ABOUT 1 ¹/₂ CUPS/350 ML

Ghee is butter that has been simmered and the milk solids are removed, leaving pure butter, fat or ghee (the Hindi word for fat).

There is a slight difference between clarified butter and ghee. Ghee is simmered longer to brown the milk solids and add a slightly nutty flavor.

Clarified butter and ghee are preferable for high-heat cooking, as both have a higher smoke point and don't burn as easily as butter.

Making it is quite easy!

INGREDIENTS

1 lb/455 g unsalted butter, from grass-fed cows

COOKING INSTRUCTIONS

Using a medium-sized saucepan, melt butter over very low heat. It will start to separate into components. Let it simmer until you see a layer of foam at the top; this could take 30–60 minutes. When it seems like no more foam is rising, take the butter off the heat and use a ladle to skim off the foam. Using a sieve covered with cheesecloth, pour the butter fat through the cheesecloth into a glass storage bottle. All the milk solids will be left behind. You should have a translucent, pure butterfat. Ghee can be stored in the refrigerator or on the countertop.

HORSERADISH

MAKES ABOUT ½ CUP/120 ML

Like most packaged foods, some brands of prepared horseradish have some questionable ingredients. Luckily, making your own from horseradish root is very easy! Homemade horseradish will last in the refrigerator for 3 to 4 weeks.

INGREDIENTS

4–5-inch/10–12-cm long piece of horseradish root, peeled and chopped

6 tbsp/90 ml filtered water

1 tbsp/15 ml white vinegar

¼ tsp sea salt

COOKING INSTRUCTIONS

Place the horseradish pieces in a food processor. Add a tablespoon/15 ml of water. Keep adding water by the tablespoon/15 ml until the horseradish is well ground. You may need more or less water. Be careful: Ground up horseradish is potent, almost like chopped onions. If your mixture gets too liquidy, strain some of the water. Add a tablespoon of vinegar and salt and continue to pulse to combine. Transfer the horseradish to an airtight jar. It will keep in the refrigerator for 2 to 3 weeks.

CHEF'S TIP
The vinegar will stabilize the degree of hotness. If you prefer hot horseradish, wait a minute or two; if you prefer mild, add vinegar right away.

FLAVORED BUTTERS

MAKES 1 CUP

I keep flavored butters in the freezer and use them to fancy up simple meals like a roast, grilled steak or panfried fish. They can transform a simple meal into a special meal. You can make flavored butters with just about anything in your fridge, but here are some of my favorite combinations.

INGREDIENTS

FOR JALAPEÑO CILANTRO BUTTER:

8 oz/230 g butter, softened

1 jalapeño, minced

3 tbsp/8 g cilantro, minced

1 garlic clove, roasted and minced

1 tsp/5 g lemon zest

1 tbsp/15 ml fresh lemon juice

FOR HERB BUTTER:

8 oz/230 g unsalted butter, softened

⅛ tsp sea salt

1 tbsp/3 g each fresh parsley, basil, chervil, chopped

1 tsp/1 g fresh oregano

squeeze of fresh lemon juice

FOR SUN-DRIED TOMATO BUTTER:

8 oz/230 g unsalted butter, softened

3 tbsp/30 g sun-dried tomatoes, chopped

⅛ tsp sea salt

1 small garlic clove, roasted

1 tsp/1 g smoked paprika

FOR ANCHOVY BUTTER:

8 oz/230 g unsalted butter, softened

4 anchovies, chopped

2 garlic cloves, roasted

3 tbsp/8 g flat-leaf parsley, chopped

3 tbsp/35 g green olives, chopped

pinch of dried red pepper

COOKING INSTRUCTIONS

Combine all ingredients for each type of butter and use your hands to mix ingredients until well combined. Roll into a log shape, wrap in parchment paper and store in the fridge.

CHEF'S TIP

Make several varieties, store in ice-cube trays and use whenever your meal needs a hit of flavor!

MANGO SALSA

SERVES 4–6

This simple salsa can be served with my coconut shrimp appetizer (Coconut Shrimp with Mango Salsa, page 50), and also is excellent with roasted or grilled fish.

INGREDIENTS

1 jalapeño, seeded and minced

1 ripe mango, peeled, pitted and diced

1 tbsp/10 g red onion, chopped

1 tbsp/3 g cilantro, chopped

½ tbsp mint, chopped

¼ tsp red chili flakes

1 tbsp/15 ml fresh lime juice

1 tbsp/15 ml extra-virgin olive oil

¼ tsp sea salt

⅛ tsp pepper

COOKING INSTRUCTIONS

Combine all salsa ingredients in a medium bowl. Adjust salt and pepper to taste.

FIERY FRUIT SALSA

SERVES 6–8

Though Fiery Fruit Salsa used to be my favorite salsa, I hadn't made it in years because it called for a chipotle pepper in adobo sauce. The ingredients in canned chipotle peppers are often questionable; some even contain wheat flour. This salsa would not be the same without these smoky peppers, which I now make from scratch (Chipotle Peppers in Adobo Sauce, page 214).

The smoky heat of the chipotle pepper perfectly complements the sweetness of the pineapple perfectly.

INGREDIENTS

2 cups/400 g chopped fresh pineapple

2 Roma tomatoes, chopped

1 small red onion, diced (approximately ¼ cup/40 g)

1 chipotle pepper in adobo sauce (page 214), finely chopped

1 tbsp/15 ml of adobo sauce

2 tbsp/30 ml extra-virgin olive oil

juice of 1 orange

juice of ½ lime

2 large avocados, chopped

COOKING INSTRUCTIONS

Combine all ingredients, except avocado, in a medium-sized bowl. When all ingredients are combined, fold in avocado without smashing.

CHIPOTLE LIME VINAIGRETTE

MAKES ½ CUP/ 120 ML

This is a perfect dressing to spice up a simple fajita salad.

INGREDIENTS

2 limes, juiced

1 tsp/7 g raw honey

1 clove garlic, crushed

zest of a lime

⅛ tsp cumin

⅛ tsp chili powder

2 tbsp/5 g cilantro, minced

¼ cup/60 ml extra-virgin olive oil

sea salt and pepper to taste

COOKING INSTRUCTIONS

In a small bowl, whisk together lime juice, honey, garlic, lime zest, cumin, chili powder and cilantro. Slowly whisk in olive oil. Add salt and pepper to taste.

HERBED BALSAMIC VINAIGRETTE

MAKES ABOUT 1 CUP/236 ML

We make fresh balsamic vinaigrette weekly. The dressing is quick to make and the herbs brighten up a simple green salad.

INGREDIENTS

¼ cup/60 ml and 2 tbsp/30 ml balsamic vinegar

1 tsp/5 ml stone-ground mustard

½ tsp sea salt

½ tsp pepper

1 tbsp/3 g parsley, minced

2 tsp/40 g chives, minced

1 tsp/1 g tarragon, minced

½ cup/120 ml extra-virgin olive oil

COOKING INSTRUCTIONS

In a medium bowl, whisk together balsamic vinegar, mustard, salt, pepper and herbs. Slowly whisk in olive oil. Adjust salt and pepper to taste.

CHEF'S TIP
For best results use high-quality olive oil and vinegar.

HOMEMADE MAYONNAISE

MAKES ABOUT 1 CUP/120 ML

There are a variety of ways to make homemade mayonnaise, but this one is my favorite. The key to making a good homemade mayonnaise is to use a mild-tasting extra-virgin olive oil.

INGREDIENTS

1 egg yolk, room temperature

1 tsp/5 ml Dijon mustard

1 tbsp/15 ml lemon juice

¼ tsp sea salt

¼ tsp pepper

1 cup/240 ml mild-tasting extra-virgin olive oil

COOKING INSTRUCTIONS

Place the egg yolk, mustard, lemon juice, salt and pepper in the bowl of a food processor fitted with the blade. While it's running, add the olive oil to the insert. The insert should have a tiny hole in it that will allow the oil to slowly drip into the food processor. Leave the food processor running until all of the oil has dripped through. This emulsification process is key when making mayonnaise. Adjust salt and pepper to taste.

HOMEMADE CURRIED MAYONNAISE

MAKES ABOUT 1 CUP/120 ML

This mayonnaise tastes fantastic in an Asian-inspired chicken salad or Curried Cabbage Salad (page 135).

INGREDIENTS

1 egg yolk, room temperature

1 tsp/5 ml stone-ground mustard

1 tbsp/15 ml fresh lemon juice

¼ tsp sea salt

¼ tsp pepper

1 cup/240 ml mild-tasting extra-virgin olive oil

1 tsp/1 g mild curry powder

COOKING INSTRUCTIONS

Place the egg yolk, mustard, lemon juice, salt and pepper in the bowl of a food processor fitted with the blade. While it's running, add the olive oil to the insert. The insert should have a tiny hole in it that will allow the oil to slowly drip into the food processor. Leave the food processor running until all of the oil has dripped through. This emulsification process is key when making mayonnaise. Add the curry powder and give the food processor a quick whirl. Adjust salt and pepper to taste.

HOMEMADE WASABI MAYONNAISE

MAKES ABOUT 1 CUP/120 ML

For a quick and healthy appetizer, drizzle this mayonnaise over Smoked Salmon Nori Wraps (page 37).

INGREDIENTS

1 egg yolk, room temperature

1 tsp/5 ml stone-ground mustard

1 tbsp/15 ml fresh lemon juice

¼ tsp salt

¼ tsp freshly ground black pepper

1 cup/240 ml mild-tasting extra-virgin olive oil

2 tsp/2 g wasabi powder

pinch of cayenne

COOKING INSTRUCTIONS

Place the egg yolk, mustard, lemon juice, salt and pepper in the bowl of a food processer fitted with the blade. While it's running, add the olive oil to the insert. The insert should have a tiny hole in it that will allow the oil to slowly drip into the food processor. Leave the food processor running until all of the oil has dripped through. This emulsification process is key when making mayonnaise. Add the wasabi powder and cayenne and give the food processor a quick whirl. Adjust salt and pepper to taste.

CHEF'S TIP
Read labels carefully and make sure that the wasabi powder is 100 percent wasabi and does not have other ingredients added.

ACKNOWLEDGMENTS

TO BROOKE, MY HUSBAND

Thank you for putting up with and loving my workaholic ways. Thank you for being so understanding of my lack of time to socialize, relax and spend time together throughout this book-writing process. Thank you for being the most amazing father to Indyanna and spending all of your time off with her so I could cook, write and research. Thank you for testing every recipe in this book and providing honest feedback. Mostly, thank you for always being supportive and having complete faith in my ability to succeed.

TO EDA, MY MOM

Thank you for being my sous-chef, my prep cook, my dishwasher, my nanny. This book could have never happened without your tremendous amounts of help and support. I love you, mom!

TO INDYANNA, MY DAUGHTER

Thank you for being you—an extremely curious and independent little person! Some of my favorite moments as a mother have been glancing over from the kitchen and observing how enthralled you are in your play. You have taught me the true importance of living life presently. You are the happiest person I know. I have no doubt that you will grow up to do great things.

TO TARYN, MY DEAR FRIEND

Thank you for more-than-gently nudging me, some might call it pressuring me, to start my blog. Without your encouragement, I wouldn't be doing what I love today. Thank you for the many heart-to-hearts about life, careers and following our passions. You have been one of my biggest inspirations!

TO CHRIS KRESSER

Thank you for all that you do. I would not be doing this project if it were not for your practice and your investigative medicine approach. Before working with you, I spent a decade in doctors' offices to no avail. I cannot thank you enough for helping me regain my health and, in turn, my passion for cooking!

TO AMY KUBAL

Thank you for being such a fantastic partner on this project, as well as on my previous cookbook. I have learned so much through our exchanges. You really are the best!

TO LIZ WOLFE

I have learned so much from your blog, your podcast and our email exchanges. Your blog posts are what encouraged me to extend my Paleo lifestyle from my kitchen to my skin care and beyond. I am so inspired by the business you have built around educating and helping others. I adore the enthusiasm, passion and wit that you bring to the Paleo community. I am so honored that you agreed to write the foreword to my book. Thanks a million!

TO WILL KIESTER AND THE PAGE STREET PUBLISHING TEAM

Thank you for the opportunity to write this cookbook and share my culinary creations and my passion for healthy living with others. And thank you for guiding me through the book-writing process.

TO MY FRIENDS AND FAMILY

Thank you for the overwhelming love, support and encouragement you have provided. Thank you for being understanding of my absence throughout this process. I look forward to spending more time with you and sharing healthy meals!

TO THE VGN BLOGGERS

Thank you for the inspiration, motivation and support. The community you've provided has made the grueling process of writing a book while balancing all of my many other life responsibilities much more pleasant. I have learned a tremendous amount from all of you. Every day, I am motivated and inspired by you to keep following my passions.

TO MY BLOG READERS

Thank you so much for following my story and my adventures in the kitchen! Receiving emails and kind notes from you when I am overwhelmed, stressed and feeling like a chicken with my head cut off reminds me why I love doing what I do.

ABOUT THE AUTHOR

ARSY VARTANIAN is the founder of the Paleo recipe and lifestyle blog Rubies and Radishes and the author of the best-selling cookbook *The Paleo Slow Cooker*.

In an effort to achieve optimal health and wellness, she discovered CrossFit and the Paleo diet in 2008. Arsy started feeling better than ever and was eventually able to recover from health issues that she had struggled with for almost a decade.

She is also a home cook who deeply enjoys spending time in her kitchen and creating healthy, grain-free recipes for her family and her blog readers.

Arsy resides in the beach town of Santa Cruz, California, with her wonderful husband and amazing daughter.

INDEX